Silent S

by

Nardos Tesfagabr

MAPLE
PUBLISHERS

Silent Suffering

Author: Nardos Tesfagabr

Copyright © Nardos Tesfagabr (2023)

The right of Nardos Tesfagabr to be identified as author of this work has been asserted by the author in accordance with section 77 and 78 of the Copyright, Designs and Patents Act 1988.

First Published in 2023

ISBN: 978-1-915996-64-0 (Paperback)
       978-1-915996-65-7 (eBook)

Book cover and Book layout by:

White Magic Studios
www.whitemagicstudios.co.uk

Published by:

Maple Publishers
Fairbourne Drive, Atterbury,
Milton Keynes,
MK10 9RG, UK
www.maplepublishers.com

Contents

Introduction

Do you ever take your safety, security, and basic needs for granted? What if your very existence was a daily struggle for survival? What if you lived in a world where every day was a battle just to stay alive?

Asmara, the capital city of Eritrea, is known for its striking architecture and vibrant street life. But for the people who call this city home, life is anything but easy. I should know - I was born in Eritrea, and I grew up surrounded by the sights, sounds and smells of this beautiful, complicated city.

But as I got older, I began to realize that my experiences were vastly different from those of people in other parts of the world. While others took their safety, security, and even their basic needs for granted, I knew that every day was a struggle just to survive.

In this book, I want to shed light on the struggles of Eritreans and compare them to those of people in other parts of the world. What does it mean to live in a place where water is scarce, food is scarce, and access to healthcare is almost non-existent? What does it mean to live in a country where political oppression and human rights abuses are a daily reality?

But this is not just a book about struggle. It is also a book about hope. Despite the many obstacles that Eritreans face, they continue to find ways to thrive, connect, and build a better future for themselves and their communities. I hope that by reading this book, you will come away with a greater sense of the challenges we face as a global community, but also with a greater sense of our shared humanity and our capacity for compassion, resilience, and hope.

Governments have frequently engaged in conflict and war throughout history to improve the lives of their populations. This has frequently meant warring with other countries or organizations to seize resources or win unfamiliar territory. In Eritrea, however, the government has chosen to act against its people, causing great suffering and a significant lack of fundamental freedoms.

The People's Front for Democracy and Justice (PFDJ), a political party that has tightly controlled all facets of the nation's political and social life, has dominated Eritrea since it gained independence from Ethiopia in 1993. To create a strong and independent country, the government has justified its oppressive tactics; yet, in practice, these measures have only worked to stifle opposition and uphold the status quo.

The national service program, which obliges all Eritreans, male, and female, to serve in the military for an indeterminate amount of time, has been one of the main ways the government has tried to control its people. The program was initially put in place as a reaction to the nation's persistent border conflicts with Ethiopia, but it has since been prolonged indefinitely, forcing many conscripts to serve for years on end, sometimes in difficult and dangerous circumstances.

Soldiers frequently engage in forced labour, get little pay, and have restricted access to food and water while serving in the military, making their living conditions notoriously bad. Moreover, harsh penalties, including incarceration, torture, and forced labour, are frequently meted out to individuals who voice their disapproval or try to escape the program. National service has had a disastrous effect on society, forcing many young people to give up their education and future aspirations to serve in the military. Soldiers have been sent as part of the program to keep an eye on and manage civilian populations, which has also functioned as a means of implementing the government's oppressive policies.

The Eritrean government has frequently violated human rights, especially via the use of national service, torture, and limitations on the right to free expression and assembly. People now face penalties for expressing their thoughts or criticizing the government's actions, creating an atmosphere of fear and repression. The acts of the government have significantly impacted Eritreans' life; many have been driven to leave the nation in pursuit of safety and freedom. Eritreans are now widely dispersed over the globe, many living apart from their families and attempting to start over in strange and foreign environments. This has resulted in a sizable diaspora group.

The Eritrean government has argued that its policies are essential for the growth and security of the nation, but in practice, they have resulted in widespread suffering and a lack of fundamental freedoms. Young people's lives have been profoundly impacted by the employment of national service as a population control tool; many of them have been compelled to give up their ambitions and aspirations to spend an indeterminate amount of time in the military. In addition to instilling fear and intimidation, the government's violations of human rights have led to people being punished for voicing their thoughts or criticizing its policies.

The government of Eritrea's activities has worked to erode the rights and liberties of its people, causing great hardship and a serious lack of fundamental liberties. While governments have frequently waged war and participated in struggles to improve the lives of their population throughout history, the Eritrean government has instead targeted its people, with disastrous results. The international community must intervene to protect the rights and well-being of all Eritreans and to make the government responsible for its deeds. The nation can only start to advance towards a more equitable and democratic society, one that appreciates the dignity and worth of all people, via consistent and concerted efforts.

In addition, the actions of the Eritrean government have destroyed the nation's infrastructure and economy, making it impossible for the populace to get needs like food and clean water. Widespread poverty and starvation have resulted from the government's failure to address these problems, especially in rural regions.

The Eritrean government has also been charged with utilizing forced labour to complete its projects, including constructing roads and dams. Young people are sometimes compelled to labour on these projects in difficult and hazardous conditions for little to no remuneration. Individuals who refuse to labour or try to flee risk harsh penalties, such as incarceration and torture. Many Eritreans have left the nation, and many of them risked their lives to do so, because of the government's disrespect for human rights and the welfare of its people. The United Nations estimates that 5,000 people leave Eritrea each month, many of them are undertaking the perilous voyage to Europe through the Mediterranean Sea and Sahara Desert. Several people pass away end route through hunger, thirst, and violence.

The international world, notably the UN and human rights organizations, has strongly denounced the acts of the Eritrean government. Despite this, the administration has carried on as usual with impunity, showing no indications of progress or reform. The policies and actions of the Eritrean government have destroyed the nation and caused its citizens to suffer, in conclusion. Young people have left in droves, and the nation's human resources have been depleted because of the government's contempt for human rights, freedom of speech, and citizen welfare. The moment has come for the world community to intervene and make the Eritrean regime responsible for its crimes against humanity.

Chapter 1
What are Human Rights?

The idea of human rights is more than just a dry, factual subject. It is a sensitive, significant topic that has an impact on everyone in the world. Human rights are about the fundamental rights that each person has because of their humanity. These are universal and hold for everyone, regardless of their background or identity.

The concept of human rights has changed and broadened over history to include a variety of concerns. These days, civil and political rights, economic, social, and cultural rights, and collective rights are all regarded to be fundamental components of international law and governance. These rights are interrelated and interdependent, thus defending one right sometimes necessitates defending others.

The Universal Declaration of Human Rights is one of the most significant texts in the history of human rights (UDHR (Universal Declaration of Human Rights)). The UDHR, which was adopted by the UN General Assembly in 1948, lists the fundamental rights to which every person is entitled. They include, among others, the rights to education, labour, and the freedom of thought, conscience, and religion. They also encompass the right to life, liberty, and the protection of one's person. A key text that establishes the benchmark for human rights all around the globe is the UDHR. Notwithstanding the advancements achieved in defending and advancing human rights, significant abuses continue to occur in many regions of the world. One such nation where human rights are routinely violated is Eritrea, where the government is charged with several offenses such as repression of the right to free expression, association, and assembly as well as the use of arbitrary imprisonment, torture, and forced labour.

Both puzzling and tragic, the situation in Eritrea. There are no independent media outlets in the nation because of the government's strict control over the media and restriction on any independent press. Political parties other than the PFDJ, which is in power, are prohibited, and the freedom of organization and assembly is severely constrained. Religious leaders, particularly those from unregistered religious groups, have been detained and religious institutions have been shut down.

Arbitrary imprisonment, torture, and forced labour are among Eritrea's most serious human rights violations. Tens of thousands of political prisoners are said to be held in detention facilities, and the government frequently imprisons people without giving them a chance to defend themselves in court. According to reports, captives in Eritrean detention facilities are frequently subjected to torture, including beatings, electric shocks, and other types of physical and mental abuse. In Eritrea, where the government enforces a system of mandatory national service that compels residents to serve in the military or other official capacities for extended lengths of time, forced labour is a fundamental problem as well. Human rights abuses have numerous, complicated causes, yet some things may be done to make things better. Advocacy, education, and awareness-building are essential for advancing human rights and holding governments responsible for their deeds. Furthermore, international human rights organizations like the United Nations and regional human rights organizations are crucial in observing and responding to human rights breaches.

Human rights are more than just a political or legal concern. They demand our attention and participation because they are a crucial and very emotional aspect of our humanity. Recognizing the interconnectivity of human rights and the necessity of defending and advancing them everywhere in the globe is essential. By doing this, we can build a society in which everyone's human rights, irrespective of background, are recognized and preserved.

Our society's foundation is human rights. These are the fundamental rights that every person has by being a human being. No matter a person's colour, ethnicity, gender, religion, language, or any other characteristic, it is morally required that we support their rights.

As the idea of human rights has developed, it is now understood that they are a fundamental component of international law and government. For the creation of a just and equal society in which each person may live with respect and dignity, human rights must be protected and promoted.

Equal chances and values are due to each of us. There should never be a distinction between us, and prosperity and pleasure based on our color, gender, ethnicity, religion, or any other status. Regrettably, there are still many individuals suffering from injustice and discrimination, and their human rights are being infringed. This is a problem that affects everyone; it is not just about personal pain. When certain people are denied their rights, our society is weakened, and we all suffer as a result. We must assist people who do not have the same rights and freedoms that we possess as members of the global community. We have a moral responsibility to fight for justice and equality and to raise our voices against violations of human rights wherever they take place. By doing this, we can improve the lives of countless numbers of people and make the world a more just and equal place for everybody.

Raising awareness and inspiring action are two of the biggest obstacles to promoting and safeguarding human rights. We must all become knowledgeable about human rights and the significance of defending them. By different tactics, such as taking part in rallies, signing petitions, or contacting our elected officials, we may advocate for change.

Monitoring and responding to human rights abuses is a key responsibility of international human rights mechanisms like the United Nations and regional human rights agencies. These systems give people and organizations a forum to denounce wrongdoing and request compensation for human rights breaches.

Human rights are therefore more than simply a theoretical idea; they play a crucial role in our society. We are all entitled to live in dignity and with respect, and we must see to it that everyone enjoys this right. We can build a more just, fair, and caring world by advancing and defending human rights. We can change things and create a better future for everyone if we work together.

Chapter 2
The Conscription Camps

President Isaias Afwerki

Forced labour is still a serious violation of human rights in many nations. This is seen in Eritrea, where the leadership justifies national service conscription as a necessary precaution to defend the nation from foreign threats, notably Ethiopia. The truth is that most Eritreans saw national service as an unpaid kind of forced labour with no end in sight.

This approach has an especially negative effect on young people because they are frequently drafted just after they graduate from high school. Many of these young people attempt to escape the country at tremendous personal risk to evade national service but are exposed to severe and hazardous conditions, including torture and abuse They frequently suffer harsh punishments for trying to flee, such as incarceration and torture.

This human rights violation has had a significant impact on the Eritrean people and wide-ranging repercussions. Many Eritreans are prevented from achieving their objectives and aspirations due to the restriction of independent media, arbitrary incarceration, torture, and forced labour. A considerable number of refugees have also fled the nation because of the violation of human rights; it is believed that 5,000 individuals do so each month. These migrants are frequently compelled to flee to neighbouring nations where they will experience more prejudice and persecution. The circumstance in Eritrea emphasizes the value of human rights for all individuals as well as the necessity of ongoing attention and effort to safeguard these rights. The international community must condemn the Eritrean government for its abuse of human rights and to aid Eritreans in defending their freedoms and rights. Examples of the effects of forced labour in Eritrea in real life include the experience of Samson, a young man who was compelled to serve in the national service at the age of 18. He endured torture and violence while serving in the military, including being beaten and having his arms hung from a tree. In addition, he was made to labour long hours for no compensation and was prohibited from leaving the camp. He attempted to flee but was apprehended and held captive for three months. Another illustration is the tale of Rahel, a young lady who was drafted into the military at the age of 20. She was compelled to work long hours in a factory without being paid and was not allowed to escape. She was compelled to keep working when she was ill and was not allowed to receive medical attention. She managed to flee and is currently living as a refugee in Sudan.

These instances highlight the serious effects of forced labour and human rights abuses in Eritrea and the immediate need for action to safeguard everyone's freedoms and rights. Eritrean teenagers are compelled to serve forever in these conscription camps, with no end in sight. They endure arduous physical work and military training while receiving little to no pay or fundamental human rights. The government claims that this service is essential to safeguarding the nation from foreign threats, but the truth is that young people are frequently detained in isolated areas that are dangerous and unsafe, where they must endure difficult living conditions, sweltering temperatures, and the constant threat of violence.

The fact that there is no way out of Eritrea's conscription system is among its most alarming features. Once drafted, a person cannot leave the military or go home without getting permission from the government, which is sometimes quite challenging to do. Unauthorized attempts to desert or flee might lead to harsh penalties including incarceration, torture, and even death.

This system has a terrible effect on young people in Eritrea. Many experiences physical and psychological stress, while others lose their lives in war or pass away from avoidable diseases because of a lack of access to basic healthcare. Some conscripts, it has been said, are made to labour in mines or on construction sites where they are exposed to hazardous substances and situations without any safety training or equipment. Others are tasked with fighting on battles' front lines, where they run the danger of dying or becoming hurt.

The Eritrean government has not demonstrated much readiness to change its policies, despite the broad condemnation of this system by the international community. To find safety and a brighter future, many young Eritreans are compelled to leave their country. In doing so, they become refugees and frequently endanger their lives.

Depending on their assignment, each person in the conscription camps has a different responsibility. Some are trained as soldiers and deployed to the front lines of hostilities, while some are compelled to perform hard labour in the fields of agriculture, mining, or construction. Conscripts are subjected to heavy punishments for disobedience or trying to escape the camp without authorization, regardless of their designated duties, and are required to work long hours with minimal relaxation. The lack of fundamental human rights and the impossibility of leaving the conditions in Eritrea's recruitment camps make it a genuine human tragedy.

Military

Many young people have fled Eritrea in pursuit of better economic and political possibilities because of the military's reputation for harsh working conditions, poor pay, and an indefinite recruitment term.

Men and women between the ages of 18 and 50 must enlist in the military, and this requirement has been in force since Eritrea's independence from Ethiopia in 1993. The conscripts are sometimes obliged to serve for lengthy periods; these stints can occasionally endure for years or even decades with no apparent end in sight.

There have been reports of exceedingly terrible living circumstances in the military camps, with little consideration for safety, cleanliness, or medical treatment. Conscripts frequently labour long hours, have a little downtime, and receive poor nourishment. Others have complained of being forced to sleep outside without shelter from the weather or being physically abused or tortured.

Many young individuals who have been recruited into the Eritrean military face physical challenges in addition to the danger of being indoctrinated. To indoctrinate soldiers and persuade them to blindly adhere to the regime's objectives and views, the government employs several propaganda techniques. This entails regulating communication channels, restricting access to outside information, and promoting a climate of fear and distrust. Conscripts are urged to spy on one another and inform the authorities of any opposing beliefs or actions, which fosters a culture of perpetual watchfulness and distrust. Defiance from the government or speaking out against its policies can have serious repercussions, and individuals who try to do so frequently face harsh punishment, such as torture and incarceration.

Several Eritreans fled the nation due to the poor wages and unfavourable living conditions in military camps. With an estimated 5,000 individuals fleeing the nation each month, Eritrea is said to have one of the highest rates of forced migration in the whole globe.

Many of these migrants face serious risks as they try to escape the nation; some are compelled to make perilous crossings of the Sahara Desert or the Mediterranean Sea in packed boats. Eritrean migrants frequently encounter further hazards and difficulties after they arrive at their destinations. Many people are compelled to live in congested, unhygienic quarters with limited access to essentials including food, water, and medical care.

They may occasionally be the targets of exploitation and abuse, including forced labour, human trafficking, and sexual assault. Eritrean women are particularly at risk since they are frequently the targets of human traffickers and are compelled to engage in prostitution or domestic slavery.

Many young Eritreans still leave their nation in pursuit of a better life despite the hazards and difficulties. People act in this way because of a desire for independence, chance, and the ability to create a better future for themselves and their families. Yet, there is no prospect of political or economic transformation in Eritrea, and the situation there remains dire. To repress opposition and keep its hold on power, the government continues to exercise strong control over the populace by employing strategies including arbitrary arrests, disappearances, and censorship.

The departure of Eritrean people is expected to continue unless major improvements are made to the country's political and economic climate. The continuous migratory problem affects the stability and security of the area as a whole and is not only a humanitarian concern. Ciham Ali Abdu's detention in 2012 at the age of 15 as she tried to escape the nation with her family is another illustration of the toughest penalties in Eritrea. She was tortured physically and mentally as she was held in custody for more than six years without being charged or going through a trial. Abdu was detained for protracted periods without communication and was not allowed to get medical care or legal counsel. She endured beatings, electric shocks, and other sorts of abuse while being detained in isolation. She was held until November 2020, when she was freed from prison and put under house arrest, despite several requests for her release from international human rights organizations and the United Nations. The case of Ciham Ali Abdu brings to light how the Eritrean government uses torture and arbitrary detention as tactics of repression. It also highlights the country's vulnerable youth, who are frequently subjected to compulsory military service and other types of governmental violence. Many young people from Eritrea still leave the nation in quest of safety and a better future despite the hazards, encountering many perils and difficulties in the process.

In Eritrea, forced labour is another frequent form of punishment in addition to torture and extended incarceration. All citizens between the ages of 18 and 50 are required to participate in the military or other state-run programs as part of the government's national service program. The periods of service are frequently illimitable and may endure for years or even decades, with people being sent to work in a variety of sectors, including manufacturing, mining, construction, and agriculture.

Many people who are drafted into the national service program labour under unfavourable circumstances, including as long hours, meager compensation, and restricted access to food, drink, and medical care. Others are made to labour in dangerous conditions without the necessary safety gear or training, which can lead to accidents and even fatalities.

Forced labour is allegedly being employed by the government as a method of population control and resource extraction from the populace. Several Eritreans have left the country to avoid the hardships associated with the national service program. Individuals are penalized for expressing their thoughts or challenging the government's policies in Eritrea, which has overall resulted in a culture of fear and repression. This has significantly impacted the nation's human rights record and caused great human suffering. Despite these obstacles, many Eritreans continue to put their lives in danger for the sake of a more equitable and democratic country.

The idea of leaving Eritrea is terrifying and perilous for many of its citizens. Without the appropriate documents, those who try to leave the nation run the possibility of being detained and incarcerated, and upon their return, sometimes face harsh punishment. Because of this, many have turned to criminal avenues like people trafficking and smuggling networks, which may be risky and expensive.

The International Organization for Migration estimates that 36,000 Eritreans crossed the Mediterranean Sea into Europe in 2018, with thousands more making the effort annually. Many of these people encounter terrifying circumstances along the road, such as exploitation by smugglers, mistreatment by security personnel, and the risks of the voyage itself. Young people are in a particularly bad condition since they frequently have no choice but to leave the nation to escape being drafted for the national service program. Many people travel alone, without the safety of family or friends, and are therefore at risk of abuse and exploitation throughout the whole voyage.

Despite these dangers, many Eritreans are adamant about leaving their country in search of freedom and the opportunity to better their lives and the lives of their families. They frequently encounter antagonism and distrust and come into difficulties at every step. The international community must acknowledge the violations of human rights occurring in Eritrea and to intervene to safeguard the rights and welfare of its population. Together with helping people who have fled the nation, this also entails attempting to make the Eritrean government responsible for its deeds.

Thus, Eritrea continues to be a nation where fundamental freedoms are lacking, and human rights are violated. There is now a culture of fear and repression due to the employment of harsh punishments including torture, indefinite incarceration, and forced labour. People now risk punishment for speaking out against the government or criticizing its policies. Many Eritreans fear that trying to leave their nation may put them in danger and put them at risk of being imprisoned, exploited, and abused. Many people continue to put their lives in danger in the pursuit of a more equal and democratic society despite these obstacles. All Eritreans' rights and well-being must be preserved, and the international community must intervene to support their efforts.

Chapter 3
Education

It is commonly acknowledged that education is a key component of societal advancement and development. Education is crucial to humanity because it allows us to learn, develop, and think critically. This essay's main goal is to examine the value of education and how it might advance individuals and civilizations.

One of the most important advantages of education is empowerment. It equips people with the knowledge and abilities to take charge of their life by enabling them to make wise decisions. For individuals who are living in poverty, education is especially crucial because it may help them escape the cycle of poverty by giving them the skills, they need to land better employment and raise their standard of life. For people to take an active role in their communities and the larger society, education is crucial. Participating in the democratic process and being aware of one's rights and obligations are essential. In nations with authoritarian administrations, education may also be a potent weapon for advancing democracy and human rights.

Economic growth is yet another crucial component of schooling. Economic growth depends on a skilled labour force that enables companies to compete and innovate on a global scale. By giving people the ability to land better-paying employment, education helps to lessen economic disparity. Empowering people with the knowledge and abilities to launch enterprises, get loans, and provide economic possibilities, also plays a significant role in eliminating poverty. Education may be a vital instrument for fostering economic progress and eradicating poverty in emerging nations.

Education is important for both professional and personal growth. People may expand their intellectual and creative potential, experiment with novel concepts and methods of thinking, and hone the critical thinking abilities needed for success in a variety of spheres of life. Education is a potent instrument for self-discovery and personal growth, aiding in the exploration of new interests and passions as well as the development of a sense of direction and purpose. Education also inspires people to practice social responsibility and have a beneficial influence on their surroundings, both locally and globally. Education also has positive effects on one's health. More educated people are more likely to embrace healthy behaviours like exercising frequently and following a healthy diet, according to studies. The ability to navigate the healthcare system and advocate for one's health is another way that education helps people receive better healthcare. Education may also improve public health by giving people the information and abilities they need to understand and deal with problems like disease outbreaks and environmental dangers. A culture of health and wellness may be developed in cultures and communities with the aid of education, which is important for enhancing the general public's health. Also, education is crucial for fostering social stability and togetherness. It fosters tolerance and acceptance by giving people the information and abilities to comprehend and value various cultures and points of view. By encouraging a more inclusive and varied society, education can aid in the reduction of prejudice and discrimination. By giving people the skills, they need to comprehend and address difficult social and political issues, encouraging communication and understanding between various groups, reducing violence, and fostering greater social and economic equality, education may also contribute to peace and security.

In conclusion, education is essential for societal and individual progress, as well as for economic expansion and social harmony. It gives people the authority and resources they need to make wise decisions, take charge of their lives, and make a positive impact on their communities and the wider world.

Eritrea has one of the lowest rates of literacy in the world due to a variety of issues with its educational system. Lack of funding, obsolete curricula, and restricted access to education, particularly for girls and underprivileged groups, are characteristics of the educational system. This essay explores these issues in depth and examines their effects considering the previously mentioned, more general advantages of education.

A significant dearth of resources plagues the Eritrean educational system, and the government makes few investments in it. Schools frequently lack essential resources, like experienced teachers, textbooks, and classroom supplies, which makes it difficult for pupils to study in comfortable settings. Furthermore, the antiquated curriculum places little emphasis on critical thinking or problem-solving and primarily emphasizes memorization and rote learning, which hinders the growth of human capital and global competitiveness.

Many children in rural regions do not have access to schools, and those who do must travel great distances and endure subpar conditions. Access to education is a major concern. Rural pupils are not afforded the same chances as their urban counterparts due to the large urban-rural gap that has been exacerbated by the centralized educational system. Girls and other marginalized groups are also greatly disadvantaged because of cultural and societal pressures that drive them out of school, into early marriages, and acts of gender-based violence. Language hurdles, prejudice, and poverty all contribute to the restricted access that children from disadvantaged groups have.

The difficulties Eritrea's education system faces have a significant impact and prevent pupils from receiving the advantages of education described in the preceding article. Students are unable to get the information and skills necessary to take charge of their lives and make educated decisions. Also, the country's economic development is being hampered by restricted access to education, which prevents people from developing the skills required for global competitiveness. The emphasis on memorizing and rote learning also hinders students' capacity for critical and creative thought, which is necessary for success in a variety of spheres of life. Also, the inability to obtain an education prevents people from developing personally and discovering their hobbies and interests. In addition, the lack of educational opportunities undermines social cohesion and public health since people are unable to adopt healthy habits and respect various cultures and viewpoints.

Lastly, democracy and human rights are not being promoted by the educational system. Individuals are unable to participate in the democratic process because they are unable to grasp their rights and obligations due to a lack of access to education. Similarly, citizens' capacity to engage in civic society and hold leaders responsible is being hampered by out-of-date curriculum and a lack of critical thinking abilities.

The Eritrean government must emphasize the needs of underserved groups and girls by increasing its investment in education if it is to overcome these obstacles. This entails expanding educational financing, implementing inclusive and varied curricula, and enhancing access to schools in remote regions. By providing funding, advocating for legislative changes, and collaborating with the government and local communities to increase access to education and support inclusive curricula, civil society organizations, international organizations, and the private sector can all contribute significantly to Eritrea's efforts to support education. Similarly, citizens' capacity to engage in civic society and hold leaders responsible is being hampered by out-of-date curriculum and a lack of critical thinking abilities.

The Eritrean government must emphasize the needs of underserved groups and girls by increasing its investment in education if it is to overcome these obstacles. This entails expanding educational financing, implementing inclusive and varied curricula, and enhancing access to schools in remote regions. By providing funding, advocating for legislative changes, and collaborating with the government and local communities to increase access to education and support inclusive curricula, civil society organizations, international organizations, and the private sector can all contribute significantly to Eritrea's efforts to support education. Many issues with Eritrea's educational system are impeding its progress and keeping its people from reaping the rewards of education. The nation can ensure that all citizens may realize their full potential by investing in education, which also helps to advance public health, social cohesion, democracy, and human rights. To make this a reality, changes must be made, and everyone involved in Eritrea's education system must cooperate.

Sawa

After graduating from high school, all Eritrean students must participate in a compulsory military training program in Sawa. For the course of the 18-month program, the trainees are put through a demanding military training regimen that includes physical training, weapon instruction, and political indoctrination.

Several former pupils have spoken out about abuse, torture, and other degrading treatment while at Sawa, describing the conditions there as brutal and horrifying. Concerns concerning the use of forced labour and slavery-like circumstances at the camp have also been expressed by human rights organizations.

The fact that kids are compelled to participate in military training against their will without the ability to opt-out or appeal raises one of the biggest issues with

Sawa. International human rights legislation, which upholds the right to conscientious objection to military service, is seen to be violated by this practice. Many students must also put up with unfavourable living circumstances, such as congestion, uncleanliness, and insufficient food and water supplies.

There have been several allegations of abuse and mistreatment at Sawa, including cases of physical assault, sexual abuse, and torture. Past pupils have described being subjected to rape, sexual harassment, and physical abuse such as electric shocks, beatings, and other types of physical torture. In addition, a lot of students are compelled to put up with circumstances that are harmful to their bodily and mental health by being refused access to medical treatment and mental health services. Many pupils at Sawa are required to work for no compensation and are treated inhumanely, which has led to the situation there being compared to modern-day slavery. Students are routinely exposed to hazardous working conditions and utilized as forced labour in a variety of sectors, including agriculture, construction, and mining.

International human rights organizations have condemned the practice of forced labour and slavery-like circumstances at Sawa and urged the Eritrean government to defend the rights of its people by reforming its military training program. The administration, however, has steadfastly defended the use of required military training and opposed demands for change. Very troubling and constituting a grave breach of international human rights law, the situation in Sawa is. It is unacceptable to utilize forced labour, subject people to physical and mental torture, or treat them inhumanely, and the Eritrean government must act immediately now to solve these problems and defend the rights of its people. The circumstances in Sawa have also been brought up by Meron Estifanos. She explains how pupils were made to labour in the camp's farms and construction sites, sometimes for no pay and in perilous circumstances. She also discusses the sexual and physical abuse that other students endured, including rape and sexual harassment.

There have been other complaints from human rights groups concerning the torture and abuse that occurs at Sawa in addition to these individual stories. The Eritrean government has been urged to overhaul its military training program and defend the rights of its population after the UN repeatedly voiced concerns about the use of forced labour and slavery-like conditions. Yet, the Eritrean government has persisted in defending its military training program and blocking visits to the Sawa camp by foreign human rights organizations. It has been challenging to determine the entire scope of the abuses that occur at Sawa due to a lack of accountability and openness.

Students who are compelled to participate in military training against their will face serious mental health issues in addition to physical mistreatment at Sawa. As a result of their experiences, many students suffer from trauma, despair, and anxiety and are frequently refused access to mental health care. It is impossible to overstate how much the Sawa military training camp has impacted Eritreans' lives. A heartbreaking expression of Eritrea's disregard for human dignity, the widespread abuses and maltreatment that occur there constitute a grave breach of international human rights law.

Chapter 4
Prisons

Human rights organizations have serious concerns about the Eritrean prison system because of the terrible circumstances, abuse of prisoners, and absence of adequate legal safeguards. The United States Department of State's 2020 Human Rights Report states that Eritrea has more prisons than any other government sector and that these jails are overcrowded, filthy, and lacking in essentials including food, water, and medical treatment.

In Eritrea, prisoners are frequently imprisoned incommunicado, subjected to physical abuse and torture, and held for extended periods without charge or trial. They also have no access to family members or legal counsel. Political dissidents, journalists, and others who speak out against the government are silenced by the government through the employment of prisons. Also, political prisoners' families are held in custody.

The fact that Eritrea's inhabitants must conduct military or civilian duty as part of an ongoing national service requirement only serves to exacerbate the problem. Individuals who reject or attempt to leave the nation risk being detained and put in jail. According to Amnesty International, hundreds of political prisoners are now detained in Eritrea without being charged or facing a trial; others have been there for a long time.

Moreover, Eritrea maintains detention facilities for migrants and refugees, all of which feature terrible circumstances and abuse of inmates. Thousands of Eritreans who fled the nation have been forcibly brought back, only to endure incarceration, torture, and other types of persecution. The government of Eritrea has been urged to improve circumstances, release political detainees, and uphold human rights since the country's jail system lacks due process and mistreats inmates. It is challenging to find reliable information about prisoner experiences, though, as the government imposes strong restrictions on information and prevents independent media and human rights organizations from operating freely in the nation.

Despite this, tales from people who have endured hardship in Eritrea's jails are nonetheless horrifying. Journalist Dawit Isaak, a citizen of Sweden, has been detained without access to his family since 2001 because of his work for alternative media outlets. Isaak wrote to his family in 2018 to detail the conditions of his confinement, which included being detained in a cramped cell with no windows, sunlight, or fresh air, as well as being tortured physically and mentally. In Eritrea, several additional detainees have been detained similarly without being tried or given accusations. There is an urgent need for improvements in the country's jail and judicial systems, as seen by the sheer number of prisons in Eritrea, the awful circumstances inside of them, and the thousands of political prisoners kept without charges or trials. Human rights organizations continue to urge for the release of political prisoners and an improvement in the conditions of detention institutions to address the ill-treatment and lack of due process that detainees experience.

Number of prisons

Eritrea has a one-party system with a heavily concentrated executive branch. Political dissidents, journalists, and members of ethnic and religious minorities are jailed in the nation's extensive network of jails, detention facilities, and labour camps. These institutions have been linked to official accusations of torturing, raping, and killing detainees.

Eritrea really has one of the highest rates of incarceration worldwide. Human Rights Watch said that Eritrea has the highest ratio of prisons in the world, with one jail for every 14,000 residents. There have been instances of detainees being detained incommunicado, without access to legal counsel or medical care, in the nation's infamously harsh and draconian jail system. The necessity to protect national security and fight terrorism has been used by the government to defend the use of jail and detention. Nonetheless, several human rights organisations have condemned the administration for often using jail and detention to stifle political opposition and silence criticism.

Eritrea has created a system of forced labour camps where inmates are compelled to perform hard labour without compensation in addition to its jail system. These labour camps have been linked to allegations that the government uses them to stifle dissent and manage the populace.

The use of jail and detention on a large scale in Eritrea has alarmed the international community. The Eritrean government has been urged by the UN to improve its record on human rights, notably how it treats political prisoners and detainees. Nonetheless, the administration has resisted reform and has barred foreign observers of human rights from entering the nation.

Moreover, Eritrea has an alarmingly high number of jails and detention facilities compared to its size. Many jails and detention facilities are thought to exist in Eritrea, some of which are thought to be subterranean or concealed from view, according to human rights organisations.

These prisons are notorious for their harsh and brutal circumstances, with stories of sexual assault, forced labour, and torture of inmates. Many prisoners are kept incommunicado and denied access to family visits, medical attention, or legal counsel. Moreover, there are worries about enforced disappearances since the government frequently withholds information about the location or status of persons it detains.

Due to Eritrea's substantial number of jails and detention facilities as well as the government's lack of accountability and transparency, there are significant worries regarding the country's human rights situation. The African Union, the United Nations, and other international organisations have all criticised the use of detention and incarceration to stifle dissent and crush political opposition as a flagrant breach of international human rights norms.

In summary, Eritrea's huge concentration of jails and detention facilities raises serious concerns and exposes the administration's contempt for legality and human rights. The Eritrean government must be put under further pressure from the international community to preserve the rights and freedoms of all Eritreans and to improve its record on human rights.

Chapter 5
Salary and Economy

The government of Eritrea dominates the country's economy; it holds sway over most sectors and has put in place measures to increase self-sufficiency and lessen reliance on international aid. Despite the government's assertions that these measures have contributed to the development of a robust and resilient economy, many Eritreans now face elevated levels of poverty, unemployment, and a lack of basic needs.

Low pay and a dearth of employment possibilities are two of the primary problems Eritrean employees face. The International Labour Organization (ILO) estimates that Eritrea's minimum wage, which is about $30 per month, is one of the lowest in the world. For employees to afford their fundamental requirements, such as food, housing, and healthcare, this pay is insufficient. Apart from limiting access to foreign currency and outlawing private industry in many industries, the government has also established measures that limit the capacity of people to earn money from outside sources. This has limited work prospects and made it more difficult for Eritreans to create their enterprises or conduct commerce with other nations, aggravating the problem of poverty and unemployment.

Lack of needs including food, fresh water, and medical care is another problem. The World Food Programme estimates that there are about 2 million food-insecure individuals in Eritrea, many of whom are malnourished and hungry. Government rules have been put in place that restricts people's access to food and the capacity of humanitarian groups to help those in need. In Eritrea, a lot of people lack access to clean water sources and sanitary services, which is a fundamental problem. The high frequency of waterborne illnesses and other health problems is a result of this.

Eritrea's healthcare system is also woefully underfunded and deficient in essential tools and supplies. The country has one of the highest rates of maternal mortality in the world, according to the World Health Organization, and many common illnesses and injuries are not appropriately treated because of a lack of funding.

Notwithstanding these obstacles, some Eritrean experts can land well-paying employment, notably in the public sector. Yet, these positions are frequently only available to individuals with ties to the ruling party or administration. Furthermore, the prohibitive cost of living and restricted access to necessary products and services means that even individuals with well-paying employment sometimes struggle to satisfy basic needs. As the government carefully regulates the exchange rate, it is challenging for Eritreans to get foreign money or engage in international trade, which raises the cost of imported products.

Despite government efforts to create a self-sufficient economy, Eritrea's overall economic position is marked by poverty, unemployment, and a lack of essentials for many people. The nation's policies make it challenging for employees to earn a fair living and satisfy their fundamental necessities by restricting access to necessary products and services and limiting job possibilities. It can be difficult to set a minimum wage that guarantees a liveable standard of living because the cost of living and necessities differ based on geography, family size, and other demographic considerations. Nonetheless, it is possible to create a minimum wage that enables employees to cover their fundamental requirements by using several international standards and best practices.

The International Labour Organization (ILO) suggests that minimum wages be established at a level that satisfies employees' fundamental requirements for food, shelter, and healthcare as well as a "decent quality of life." The International Labor Organization (ILO) also suggests that minimum wages be determined through a process of social dialogue and consultation with employers and workers' representatives, taking into consideration economic conditions and other factors. The Eritrean minimum wage, which is now roughly $30 per month, is well below what is thought to be a respectable quality of living. A minimum wage that is at least equal to the price of a basic basket of goods and services, which includes food, housing, healthcare, education, and other essentials, should be established to ensure that employees can satisfy their fundamental needs.

The World Bank reports that the poverty line in Eritrea is around $1.9 per day or $57 per month. This shows that to give workers an acceptable quality of life, a minimum wage of at least $60 to $70 per month would be required. Setting a minimum wage is simply one step in ensuring that workers have an excellent quality of life, though. Making sure that employees have access to other fundamental requirements like housing, healthcare, and education is also crucial.

Many individuals in Eritrea, especially those who live in rural regions, have limited access to these essentials. To achieve self-sufficiency, the government has put in place rules that have restricted access to foreign aid and the capacity of relief organizations to help individuals in need.

Government spending on housing, healthcare, and education should be given priority, and efforts should be made to lower obstacles to trade and international aid. To achieve this, economic policies would need to change from encouraging self-sufficiency to encouraging economic growth and development.

The government should also endeavour to strengthen workers' labour rights and safeguards, including guaranteeing that workers have the freedom to organize and engage in collective bargaining and shielding them from discrimination and arbitrary termination. These steps would make it possible for workers to get a fair salary and work in a secure environment.

In general, ensuring that employees have a reasonable standard of living calls for a multifaceted strategy that involves establishing a minimum wage that meets workers' fundamental needs, enhancing access to basics like healthcare and education, and supporting labour rights and safeguards.

Nakfa

The nation of Eritrea is situated in the Horn of Africa. The Nakfa (ERN (Eritrea is the Nakfa)), which was created in 1997 to replace the Ethiopian Birr, is the official unit of exchange in Eritrea.

The town of Nakfa, which served as the Eritrean People's Liberation Front (EPLFstrategic)'s bastion throughout the nation's conflict with Ethiopia, bears its name. The Bank of Eritrea, the nation's central bank, is responsible for issuing the currency.

The government now controls Nakfa's exchange rate, and it is forbidden to trade the money on the black market. Foreign currency exchange for travel or other purposes might be challenging for Eritreans due to the government's strict regulations on the practice. Inflation is one of the key issues that the Eritrean economy and the Nakfa are now confronting. The country has seen substantial inflation in recent years, which has resulted in a fast rise in the cost of products and services. Due to the rising cost of living beyond their resources, many Eritreans have found it challenging to make ends meet.

The Eritrean government has tried to solve this problem by enacting a variety of economic regulations, such as import limitations and pricing controls. Nonetheless, these actions have frequently come under fire for being ineffectual and long-term harm to the economy.

The restricted convertibility of the Nakfa is another issue. It can be challenging for Eritreans to get foreign cash owing to government limitations, even though the currency is nominally convertible for various uses, like travel and international trade. The country's capacity to conduct business internationally has been hampered as a result.

Notwithstanding these difficulties, the Nakfa continues to be accepted widely across Eritrea as the official money. The government has also taken steps to strengthen the economy and stabilize the exchange rate, including spending on infrastructure and encouraging economic development.

To completely analyse the status of the Eritrean economy and currency, however, has proven challenging due to the government's lack of openness and accountability. Concerns regarding corruption and poor management in the nation have been voiced by human rights groups and other observers, which may be a factor in the difficulties the economy and the Nakfa are currently suffering.

In conclusion, the Nakfa, the currency of Eritrea, confronts a variety of difficulties relating to government policies, restricted convertibility, and inflation. Despite the government's efforts to resolve these problems, it is challenging to completely evaluate the situation due to the absence of openness and accountability in the country's economic administration and policies. Yet, the Nakfa continues to be a significant representation of the nation's independence and sovereignty, and Eritreans frequently utilize it in daily life. Many Eritreans believe that the government purposefully keeps Nakfa's exchange rate low to entice those who live abroad to bring money home to their family in Eritrea. The reasoning for this is that Eritreans working abroad would be able to send their families less money if the exchange rate were higher since the Nakfa would be worth more in foreign currency.

The fact that the Eritrean government tightly regulates the exchange rate and has a record of accomplishment of manipulating the currency for political reasons contributes to this view. For instance, the government abruptly declared all Nakfa notes exceeding a specific value worthless in 2015, citing the need for an anti-counterfeiting action. As a result of being compelled to swap their old notes for new ones at a rate that was less favourable than the market rate, many Eritreans virtually lost all their savings.

Moreover, there is evidence that the government intentionally deters Eritreans from making investments in the nation by placing limits on the repatriation of wealth and profits. This makes it challenging for Eritreans who reside abroad to make investments in the nation and can further fuel the idea that the government is more focused on collecting remittances than growing the economy.

These regulations may have a substantial effect on Eritreans residing overseas. Many Eritreans believe they have a responsibility to provide for their relatives in Eritrea, thus they may send a sizable percentage of their salary home. As a result, they could have little money left over with which to save for the future or invest in their training or professional advancement.

Furthermore, it could be challenging for Eritreans residing abroad to stay connected to their family and communities back home due to the poor currency rate. Staying in contact with loved ones and keeping a sense of connection to the nation can be challenging when the cost of travel, phone calls, and other costs is unreasonably high.

Finally, the low Nakfa exchange rate and the belief that the government purposefully manipulates the currency to promote remittances may have a considerable influence on the life of Eritreans residing abroad. While remittances may be a significant source of assistance for families in Eritrea, the government's policies may also inhibit growth and investment, which may limit the capacity of Eritreans to make investments in their future.

Chapter 6
Technology

Every area of our lives has been impacted by technology, including how we work, communicate, and access information and entertainment. Technology has transformed industries, enhanced quality of life, and created new opportunities for research and innovation. Technology has tremendous power, and it continues to profoundly influence our world.

The power of technology to link individuals across boundaries and distances is one of its most important effects. People are more linked than ever because of the development of the internet, social media, and mobile technology. Our ability to communicate, exchange information, and engage with one another has changed because of connection, creating new possibilities for cooperation and teamwork. From manufacturing and transportation to healthcare and education, technology has completely changed many sectors of the economy. It has enhanced safety and accuracy while lowering costs and making procedures more efficient. For instance, manufacturing can now make items quicker, cheaper, and more precisely than ever before because of the use of robotics and automation.

Technology has completely changed how we identify and treat problems in the field of healthcare. Genetic testing, medical imaging, and telemedicine developments have improved patient outcomes by enabling earlier and more accurate diagnosis and treatment of illnesses. Technology's capacity to democratize access to knowledge and resources is another impressive feature. People may now access a wealth of knowledge on any topic from anywhere in the globe thanks to the development of the internet. In addition to opening new prospects for social and economic growth, this has also offered new options for learning, research, and innovation.

The way we operate has also been significantly impacted by technology. The nature of employment has changed because of developments in automation, artificial intelligence, and the gig economy, opening new options for freelancers, entrepreneurs, and independent contractors. Also, it has made it feasible for employees to work remotely and communicate with one another from any location. The potential of technology to address some of the most important problems facing the world is one of its most intriguing features. Technology is creating new opportunities for innovation and problem-solving across a wide range of issues, from healthcare and poverty to climate change and energy generation. Innovations in renewable energy technology, for instance, are assisting in lowering carbon emissions and reducing the effects of climate change.

At the same time, it is critical to acknowledge that technology may have drawbacks. It can increase already-existing inequities and power disparities and be addicting and lonely. It has become increasingly challenging to separate fact from fiction as false news and disinformation have grown in popularity and worries about privacy and security remain critical issues. Technology has enormous power and has completely changed our lives. Technology has revolutionized industries, altered how people work and communicate, and produced new opportunities for cooperation, creativity, and problem-solving. Yet it is crucial to approach technology with caution and be aware of its drawbacks. By doing this, we can use technology to make the world a better place for everyone.

Yet, in Eritrea, mostly because of political and economic concerns, technology has contributed extraordinarily little to the growth of the nation. Internet and social media access has long been restricted by the government, which has tight control over information and communication technology. Eritrea thus has one of the lowest percentages of internet users in the world. Also, the nation's economic difficulties have restricted investment in innovation and technology. Eritrea's economy is mostly focused on subsistence farming and mining, and it has one of the lowest GDPs per capita in the entire world. The government has concentrated on building essential infrastructure, such as roads and power, but has made only a little amount of investment in technology and innovation.

The internet and other technologies that have revolutionized industry and communication in other areas of the world are therefore mostly unavailable to Eritreans. All media sources are under government control, and only a small number of people have access to the internet. This has made it difficult for Eritreans to communicate with the outside world and for businesspeople and inventors to produce new goods and services. Yet, there are some indications that Eritrea's technological sector is making development. The administration has stated a desire to advance information and communication technology in the nation and has started several projects to increase internet accessibility and digital literacy. To promote e-commerce and digital services and expand internet access, the government unveiled a national digital transformation strategy in 2018.

Notwithstanding these initiatives, Eritrea's technology industry still faces formidable obstacles to be addressed. The political climate of the nation, which includes a dearth of democratic institutions and severe violations of human rights, has produced a setting that is unfavourable to entrepreneurship and innovation. Building a contemporary and thriving technology sector in the nation has considerable obstacles due to its inadequate infrastructure and resources. Eritrea's restricted access to information and communication technologies has put the nation at a disadvantage in terms of economic development, innovation, and social advancement when compared to other nations with more established technology sectors. The inability of Eritreans to connect with the outside world and to obtain information and resources that may help them better their lives and communities is made possible by the absence of access to the internet and other technology.

In conclusion, even though technology has transformed the globe, political and economic reasons have limited technology's influence in Eritrea. The development of a strong and contemporary technology industry has been significantly hampered by the government's strict control over communication technologies, little investment in innovation, and low GDP per capita. Although there are some encouraging signals, Eritrea's technology industry still faces several obstacles that will take substantial reform and investment to overcome.

Eritrea's population's mental health may be significantly impacted by the country's poor access to technology and communication. Particularly, being cut off from loved ones who live overseas can cause emotions of loneliness, worry, and melancholy.

Numerous Eritreans have emigrated in quest of greater political and economic independence. Yet, many who live overseas find it challenging to stay in touch with their family and communities back home due to the government's strict control over information and communication technology. Communication is restricted to phone calls and traditional mail, which can be costly and unreliable due to the absence of internet access and social media.

As they are unable to maintain contact with their relatives and communities, Eritreans living abroad may experience tremendous stress and worry because of this loss of communication. This can be particularly challenging for people who have left behind small children or elderly family members since they cannot check on them or offer them emotional assistance while they are still far away. Lack of internet and social media access can also cause a sense of loneliness and detachment for people living in Eritrea. Eritreans are shut off from the global community in a world where technology has made it possible for people to interact and communicate across countries and time zones. This may cause a sense of isolation and a disconnect from the outer world, which may exacerbate mental health conditions like sadness and anxiety. Consequently, the public may feel despondent and helpless because of the government's control over media and information sources. Many Eritreans feel cut off from the political and social events taking place in the world around them due to limited access to information and the capacity to communicate with the outside world. This may result in a lack of agency and a sense of powerlessness in their own life, which may fuel emotions of despair and hopelessness.

Lack of access to communication and technology can have wider societal and economic effects in addition to its effect on one's mental health. Possibilities for education, economic growth, and political participation may be constrained by an inability to interact with the global community and access information and services. This can worsen mental health conditions like anxiety and depression by feeding a cycle of poverty and restricted opportunity.

In conclusion, the population's mental health may be significantly impacted by Eritrea's poor access to technology and communication. Feelings of loneliness, worry, and despair may result from being unable to communicate with loved ones who are located overseas and from not having access to information and resources. Because of the government's monopoly on information and media, many people may feel despondent and helpless, which exacerbates mental health problems. Limited access to technology has effects that go beyond a person's mental health and may worsen national social and economic problems. In addition to substantial investments in technology and communication infrastructure, addressing these issues would need more extensive political and social reforms to build a society that is open and interconnected.

Chapter 7
Destroying Houses

The Eritrean government has a lengthy history of evicting residents and destroying their homes, businesses, and industries—often without providing them with compensation or a fair trial. This behaviour has been labelled as a social control tactic, a way to amplify authority, and a way to stifle dissension.

One of the most infamous instances of this technique took place in 2003 when the government launched a drive to demolish whole neighbourhoods in Asmara, the nation's capital. There are rumours that the authorities deemed these neighbourhoods to have been built unlawfully and forced the residents to leave their houses within a few days. Those who resisted were forcibly removed, and the heavy gear was used to destroy their dwellings. As many of the affected citizens' houses and goods were destroyed in the destruction, they were left without housing and compensation. Others were compelled to transfer to government-made housing developments outside the city, many of which were subpar built and lacking necessities like electricity and running water.

The government's 2003 drive to demolish buildings as part of a larger attempt to rebuild Asmara was justified because the city's haphazard development was dangerous to the public's health and safety. Several observers, however, have condemned the effort for being used to clear land for government buildings and opulent housing projects as well as a method of retaliating against political dissidents who were seen to reside in the impacted districts.

The Eritrean government has also been charged with forcefully relocating individuals to other regions of the nation, frequently under the pretext of development or security, so this is not an unusual instance. Residents have frequently been left without any means of assistance or compensation and with little to no notice before their homes and livelihoods were destroyed.

Along with destroying dwellings over time, the Eritrean government has also expropriated and nationalized several companies. The government's takeover of all privately owned enterprises in the nation, including factories and other industrial infrastructure, in the late 1990s, is one of the most notable instances of this. This action, which was a part of a larger government drive to consolidate power and manage the economy, had a terrible effect on many Eritrean employees and business owners. As a result of the government's rigorous pricing restrictions and other rules, many firms had to close their doors or operate at a loss. As a result, many employees were fired or made to work in the informal sector of the economy, where pay and benefits are frequently subpar.

The government's strategy for industrial growth has also come under fire for lacking accountability and transparency. For instance, it has been claimed that the government has given contracts for significant infrastructure projects to foreign firms with little to no participation from Eritrean individuals or civil society organizations. This has sparked worries about nepotism and corruption and prompted some to doubt the government's commitment to sustainable development. In general, the practice of the Eritrean government of evicting residents and demolishing their houses and businesses has had a significant negative impact on many Eritreans' lives and livelihoods. Although the government has defended these moves as being necessary for security or development, many observers have denounced them as a way for the government to consolidate control and stifle opposition. As a result, many Eritreans now depend on remittances from family members overseas or the underground economy since they are without houses, employment, or other means of support.

Chapter 8
Freedom of Speech

One of the most oppressive and closed-off nations in the world is said to be Eritrea. This is mostly a result of the absence of speech freedom in the nation. The media, which includes print, radio, and television, is subject to rigorous government regulation. Many journalists and activists who dared to speak out against the dictatorship have also been locked up by it.

The absence of privately owned newspapers, radio stations, or television channels in Eritrea is one of the most well-known instances of the country's lack of free expression. The government owns every media outlet, and all journalists and editors work for the government. This implies that both the content and method of reporting are entirely under the control of the government. Reporters that cover such topics are frequently targeted for arrest, incarceration, and torture. Any reports that are critical of the government are controlled or repressed.

The Eritrean government strictly regulates the internet in addition to conventional media. With the use of sophisticated software, the government is now able to restrict access to websites that it considers to be critical of the government. Websites for news, blogs, and social media are all included in this. Because of this, Eritreans frequently must rely on state-run media channels and have limited access to independent news and information sources. The political and social climate of Eritrea has been significantly impacted by the absence of freedom of expression there. Political criticism has been muzzled and opposition groups' ability to unite and mobilize has been hampered. It has also made it challenging for regular Eritreans to voice their ideas and worries about the administration. Because of this, there is now a culture of fear and self-censorship, where individuals are reluctant to voice their minds of concern that the government would retaliate.

The absence of elections in Eritrea since 1993 is among the most glaring instances of the country's lack of freedom of speech. Although the country's constitution requires elections to be held every five years, this is the case. The ongoing war with Ethiopia and the requirement for national stability are two justifications the leadership has offered for not holding elections. Nonetheless, a lot of analysts think that the government's fear of losing control is the actual driver for the delay of elections.

The country's economic growth has been negatively impacted by Eritrea's lack of free expression. One of the world's poorest nations, Eritrea depends on remittances from its citizens who live overseas. Nonetheless, the absence of free expression has made it challenging for the nation to draw in outside capital or create a thriving private sector. The political unpredictability of the nation and the lack of openness in the government's decision-making procedures frequently deter investors and businesspeople.

In conclusion, Eritrea's lack of free expression poses a significant challenge to its political, social, and economic growth. It has cultivated a climate of fear and self-censorship, stifled political dissent, and made it hard for opposition organizations to unite and mobilize. It has also restricted access to unbiased news and information sources and made it challenging for Eritreans to voice their ideas and concerns about the administration. The country's economic development has been hampered by the government's strict control over the media and the internet, which has led to the creation of a closed society that is cut off from the rest of the world and made it challenging to draw in foreign investment and build a thriving private sector.

Adolf Hitler's Nazi dictatorship in Germany was infamous for using propaganda and subterfuge to influence the opinions and behaviour of the German people. The Nazis were able to install a culture of fear and obedience by using a combination of intimidation, disinformation, and compulsion, which made it hard for individuals to speak out against the injustice and crimes of the dictatorship. Propaganda was one of the main strategies the Nazis employed to shape the opinions of the German people. Under the direction of Joseph Goebbels, the Nazi Party made extensive use of print media, radio, motion pictures, and posters to convey its message. The propaganda was purposefully designed to play on the anxieties and prejudices of the German people to appeal to their emotions and make them more receptive to the Nazi message.

Also, the Nazis utilized terror to subjugate the German populace. This dread frequently stemmed from a sense of threat, whether it came from inside or from outside sources. By convincing the German people that they were under assault from a variety of foes, including Jews, Communists, and other unwanted groups, the Nazis instilled a sense of paranoia in their population. The severe measures of the government, including the concentration camps and the persecution of Jews and other minorities, were justified using this fear.

The Nazis' use of dissent suppression as a fundamental strategy. Because of the regime's extreme authoritarianism, all forms of dissent were mercilessly put down. The German people became fearful as a result and were reluctant to speak out against the dictatorship for fear of retaliation. Many individuals were reluctant to speak out for fear of being singled out by the Gestapo, the secret police of the Nazi administration known for its ruthless interrogation and torture techniques.

The German people's thinking was likewise subjugated by the Nazis via schooling. The administration exercised strict control over the educational system, vetting textbooks, and other educational resources to make sure they adhered to Nazi ideology. From an early age, children were taught to value their devotion to the Nazi Party and to think that the Aryan race was better. Many found it challenging to think critically and challenge the regime's policies because of this brainwashing. The cult of personality that enveloped Adolf Hitler was another element in the indoctrination of the German populace. Many Germans viewed Hitler as a hero who could take Germany to new heights because of the way he was depicted as a charismatic leader who could do no wrong. Many found it difficult to see the shortcomings of the Nazi administration or to criticize its actions because of this hero worship.

It was challenging for the German people to speak out against the injustice of the Nazi dictatorship due to a mix of propaganda, fear, repression of dissent, education, and the cult of personality that surrounded Hitler. Many individuals were reluctant to express their disagreement with the regime's policies or their opposition to the crimes being carried out. It was difficult for the opposition to grow since those who dared to voice their opinions were sometimes subject to harsh punishment. Because few Germans were ready to speak out against the government until it was too late, the Nazis were able to maintain their reign of terror for many years.

We will look at how Eritrea today is like the methods the Nazis used to mislead the German people and repress opposition.

The employment of propaganda is one of the main methods through which the Eritrean government manipulates the opinions of its people. The country's main news source is the government-controlled media, which is meticulously tailored to guarantee that the government's viewpoint is the only one heard. Also, the government has closed all independent media outlets, making it hard for individuals to receive alternate information sources. Many have found it challenging to form their ideas or to criticize the practices of the government because of this biased information flow. In addition to regulating the media, the Eritrean government has stifled opposition by instilling terror among its citizens. Those who are perceived as threats to the government's authority have a history of being arbitrarily detained and tortured by the government. To manage the populace, the government has also resorted to compulsory conscription. Young individuals are physically abused while being compelled to serve in the military for an extended length of time, sometimes years at a time. Young people find it challenging to criticize the government or launch opposition activities due to their fear of being drafted into the military. Suppression of dissent is another method used by the Eritrean government to maintain control over its populace. All opposition parties have been outlawed by the government, and anybody speaking out against it runs the possibility of being detained, tortured, or worse. Also, the government has placed onerous restrictions on civil society groups, making it challenging for them to function. People have found it challenging to unite and speak out against the government's actions as a result.

Education has also been a tool utilized by the Eritrean government to influence the minds of its people. The government maintains strict control over the educational system, and a government-approved curriculum is used to teach pupils. Also, because of government restrictions on higher education, it is challenging for young people to follow their aspirations and cultivate critical thinking abilities. Many now find it challenging to express their thoughts or criticize the policies of the government as a result.

Moreover, the cult of personality that surrounds President Isaias Afwerki is like the strategies the Nazis employed to sway the opinions of the German populace. Criticism of President Afwerki or his actions is rarely accepted since he is frequently depicted as a hero who has brought the nation to independence. As there are no term limits and the president has been in office since 1993, opposition parties find it challenging to acquire traction. The Eritrean people find it challenging to speak out against the injustice of the regime due to a mix of propaganda, fear, repression of dissent, education, and the cult of personality surrounding President Isaias Afwerki. Many people are reluctant to voice their concerns about governmental policy or to denounce wrongdoing. As those who do express dissent are frequently subject to harsh punishment, a culture of fear and submission has developed, making it difficult for dissent to grow. The strategies utilized by the Eritrean government to sway the opinions of its people are comparable to those the Nazis employed to brainwash the German populace. The government has total control over the beliefs and behaviours of its inhabitants through its use of propaganda, terror, repression of dissent, education, and the cult of personality around President Isaias Afwerki. The world community should be concerned about this perilous scenario.

Several Eritreans have departed the nation because of the repression of opposition in Eritrea, frequently in great personal danger. Around 500,000 Eritrean refugees are now living abroad, according to the United Nations. Although these refugees sometimes struggle in their new homes, many consider it to be a better situation than living under Eritrea's tyrannical government.

The international community must assist the Eritrean people and exert pressure on the administration to uphold human rights. Many assessments on the human rights situation in Eritrea have been released by the UN and other international organizations, and several nations have imposed sanctions on the Eritrean government. To remedy the problem, further work must be done.

The assistance of Eritrean civil society groups is among the most crucial things the international world can do. These groups are crucial in keeping an eye out for violations of human rights and helping those who have been hurt. Yet because of the Eritrean government's interference, several of these groups have had to shut their doors.

The international community should exert pressure on the Eritrean government to uphold human rights as another crucial action. Sanctions and public declarations are examples of diplomatic channels that can be used for this. The UN and other organizations should keep trying to record Eritrea's violations of human rights, and the international community should continue to support their efforts. We should be concerned about the situation in Eritrea. It is challenging for the Eritrean people to speak out against the injustice of the system because of the government's use of propaganda, fear, repression of dissent, education, and the cult of personality surrounding President Isaias Afwerki.

The international community must assist the Eritrean people and exert pressure on the administration to uphold human rights. We must support those who are oppressed and fight for a brighter future for everyone.

Chapter 9
Religion

Eritrea's rich and varied religious heritage reflects the history and culture of the nation. Religion has a significant impact on Eritreans' everyday life and has shaped the nation's traditions, customs, and social norms. This essay will examine the place of religion in Eritrea and how it affects its citizens.

Eritrea is a nation with a long history of religion. There are several religious communities in the nation, including adherents of conventional African faiths, Muslims, and Christians. With over 50% of the population belonging to it, the Orthodox Christian Church is the biggest religious community in Eritrea. One of the oldest and most well-established Christian churches in the world, the Eritrean Orthodox Church has had a profound impact on the history and culture of the nation.

In Eritrea, where 36% of the population practices Islam, it is the second most common religion. There are tiny Shia and Sufi populations as well as a mostly Sunni Muslim community in Eritrea. As Islam has been practiced in Eritrea for more than a thousand years, it has had a significant impact on its customs and culture.

Eritrea is home to adherents of indigenous African religions in addition to followers of Christianity and Islam. These faiths have a strong bond with nature, revere their ancestors, and hold a belief in an ultimate entity or creator. Several portions of the nation, especially rural ones, still worship traditional African faiths.

In Eritreans' daily life, religion is especially important. It plays a significant role in the cultural identity of the nation and is entwined with many facets of Eritrean life, such as language, music, and traditional clothing. Religious festivals and holidays are extensively observed throughout, and many Eritreans routinely attend religious services.

The social and cultural life of the nation is significantly influenced by the Eritrean Orthodox Church. The church has a long history of supporting social welfare, healthcare, and education, and it has been instrumental in developing the nation's infrastructure. Music, art, and literature are just a few examples of how the church has influenced Eritrean culture. The social and cultural life of Eritrea is significantly influenced by Islam. Muslims in the nation has a vibrant cultural history that includes their brand of music, dance, and architecture. The nation's Muslim populations are renowned for their warmth and solid social ties.

There have been conflicts in Eritrea between various religious groups despite the nation's extensive religious history. There have been allegations of discrimination against Muslims and adherents of indigenous African faiths, and the government has been charged with favouring the Eritrean Orthodox Church over other religious communities. Moreover, the administration has been charged with using religion to defend violations of human rights, notably those committed against journalists and political dissidents. Government crackdowns on religious organizations, Protestant and Pentecostal Christians, have been reported in recent years. The government has shut down several churches, detained pastors, and detained other religious leaders because these organizations pose a threat to the country's security.

Eritrea continues to be a deeply religious nation despite these difficulties. The country's cultural identity is fundamentally shaped by religion, which is closely entwined with its past and present. The Eritrean people continue to place a high value on their religious groups, which have contributed significantly to the development of the nation's social and cultural fabric.

Abune Antonios, the leader of the Eritrean Orthodox Church, was detained and put under house arrest by the Eritrean government in 2006. The arrest of Abune Antonios, the third Patriarch of the Eritrean Orthodox Church, the biggest religious body in the nation, was a serious setback for both the institution and its adherents.

Abune Antonios was charged by the Eritrean government with several charges, including heresy and inciting sectarian strife. The government said that he was not qualified to serve as the church's leader and that he was collaborating with foreign governments to damage Eritrea's national security.

Human rights organizations and religious authorities from all around the world have denounced the arrest of Abune Antonios. Many perceived it as an assault on religious liberty and a move by the government of Eritrea to dominate the nation's religious communities.

Abune Antonios remained under house arrest for more than ten years despite worldwide pressure, during which time his health drastically declined. His supporters said that he was detained in harsh conditions and that he was refused access to basic requirements such as medical treatment. Abune Antonios, the patriarch of the Eritrean Orthodox Church, was removed from office in 2017 and replaced by Abune Dioskoros. Supporters of Abune Antonios said that the action was politically motivated and was an effort by the government to seize control of the church.

Abune Antonios, who was 90 years old, was said to have passed while in custody in July 2019. His death is still under investigation, and no official announcement from the Eritrean government has been made on it. His backers contend that he was treated unfairly and denied medical attention, which eventually caused his death. The government of Eritrea has been repressing religious freedom there, as evidenced by the detention and torture of Abune Antonios. Religious leaders, notably those from the Protestant and Pentecostal Christian sects, have been the target of government persecution and arrest in recent years.

Moreover, the administration has been charged with using religion to defend violations of human rights, notably those committed against journalists and political dissidents. A UN report from 2019 charged the Eritrean government with systematic and pervasive violations of human rights, including arbitrary arrests and imprisonment, torture, and extrajudicial executions. These allegations have been refuted by the Eritrean administration, which also claims that it is trying to safeguard the security of the nation. Yet, several human rights groups and religious figures from all over the globe continue to criticize the government's conduct and demand that Eritrea show more respect for human rights and religious freedom.

Abune Antonios, the former leader of the Eritrean Orthodox Church, was detained and subjected to cruel treatment, which is a terrible illustration of the government's suppression of religious freedom in Eritrea. Human rights groups and religious leaders from all over the world have strongly denounced the government's actions, and there is a rising demand for the nation to respect human rights and religious freedom more. The international community must continue to keep an eye on Eritrea's human rights record and fight to hold the government responsible for its actions since the situation there is still concerning.

Chapter 10
Difficulties of Migrating

Every year, thousands of Eritreans leave their native country in search of better economic prospects, to escape political oppression, and to avoid being compelled to serve an indeterminate amount of time in the military. There, they encounter grave hazards and violations of their human rights. Many of these refugees end up in Libya.

With Muammar Gaddafi's overthrow in 2011, Libya has slid into anarchy, with competing factions fighting for control and power. Human trafficking and smuggling networks have flourished in this chaotic climate, taking advantage of the numerous refugees and migrants trying to cross the Mediterranean Sea to reach Europe. Eritreans are particularly susceptible to the risks of these voyages since they are frequently the victims of abuse such as assault, exploitation, and other types of maltreatment. According to reports, criminal gangs, and militias frequently target Eritrean refugees, kidnapping them for ransom or forcing them to work as slave laborers.

Eritrean migrants suffer hazards outside of Libya as well, in other nations where they seek asylum. As an illustration, many Eritreans have emigrated to Ethiopia, which shares a border with Eritrea. Yet in recent years, Ethiopia's leadership has come under fire for how it has handled Eritrean refugees. In 2018, the Ethiopian government decided to dismantle a camp that housed thousands of Eritrean refugees, citing security and disease-spread concerns. Human rights groups and the refugees themselves, on the other hand, stated that the action was politically motivated, and a tactic used by the Ethiopian government to put pressure on Eritrea to improve ties with Ethiopia.

Many Eritreans were left stranded when the camp, which housed over 10,000 migrants, was closed, with limited access to food, water, or medical treatment. Several of these refugees were compelled to return to Eritrea, where they ran the risk of being persecuted and subjected to various human rights cases of abuse. Some of these refugees were later transported to other camps. Human rights groups and governments from all over the globe have called for more protection for these vulnerable people in response to the suffering of Eritrean refugees. Eritreans continue to suffer risks and hazards both in their own country and when they try to escape for safety, thus the situation is still difficult.

Lampedusa tragedy

The Lampedusa tragedy refers to the deaths of more than 360 Eritrean migrants on October 3, 2013, when their boat sank off the coast of the Italian island of Lampedusa. The refugees had set out on a dangerous crossing of the Mediterranean Sea to reach Europe in hopes of a better life.

More than 500 individuals, many of them children, boarded a highly overcrowded boat in Libya and set sail for Europe. It was in bad shape and lacked essential safety features, making it extremely vulnerable to capsize. Several of the passengers were killed when they were either unable to escape the boat's lower levels in time or were thrown overboard when it began to sink.

After the tragedy, many people spoke out against the dangerous conditions that migrants suffer on their way to Europe. It also brought attention to the critical need for improved regulation and safety measures to be put in place to prevent future catastrophes of a similar nature.

The Italian government has announced a day of mourning and is conducting multiple inquiries into the incident. As a result, the tragedy has spurred discussions on immigration laws and the necessity for European countries to work together to address the underlying causes of migration and increase aid to people in need.

There is an urgent need for more action to be taken to prevent additional loss of life, and the Lampedusa tragedy serves as a sobering reminder of the hazards and perils that many migrants confront when trying to reach Europe.

In conclusion, thousands of Eritreans are compelled to leave their nation each year, sometimes in great personal danger. Many of these migrants' wind themselves up in Libya, where they are subjected to horrific risks and human rights violations at the hands of militias and criminal gangs. Eritreans seeking asylum in other nations, including Ethiopia, face additional difficulties since some governments are accused of abusing migrants and using them as players in political games. The international community must cooperate to safeguard these vulnerable populations and hold governments responsible for their actions due to the precarious circumstances confronting Eritrean refugees.

Chapter 11
Pain and Grief

Years of suffering and sadness have been experienced by the Eritrean people, mostly because of the harsh laws and practices of their government. The country's youth have suffered greatly because of the government's contempt for human rights, freedom of speech, and citizen welfare.

The forced conscription into the military, which was already mentioned, is one of the major causes of suffering and misery for Eritreans. All inhabitants of Eritrea, male and female, are obligated to serve in the military for 18 months, but the government has prolonged this obligation such that soldiers may continue to serve for years or even decades. The military requires its members to work extremely long hours for minimal compensation in challenging and sometimes dangerous circumstances. The young people of Eritrea and their families have been put under a great deal of mental and physical stress as a result.

Also, the government's habit of detaining and arresting anybody who opposes it or expresses opposition to its policies has caused a tremendous deal of suffering and anguish for Eritreans. Young people are kidnapped from their homes and locked up without a trial or access to legal counsel, shattering families. Many of them never return, leaving their families in the dark as to their whereabouts or well-being. Families that are always worried about whether they will see their loved ones again are constantly in a state of mourning.

The suppression of information and severe regulation of the media by the government adds to the suffering and anguish of the Eritrean people. Eritrea has no independent media, and all media, including radio, television, and the internet, are under government control. This indicates that the public frequently lacks knowledge of national and global affairs. Lack of information availability breeds isolation and perplexity, which exacerbates mental anguish and uncertainty.

A lot of families have experienced great anguish and sadness because of the Eritrean government's policies and actions, which have also contributed to widespread poverty and starvation. A stagnating economy and a lack of basic needs like food and clean water are the results of the government's lack of investment in the economy and infrastructure as well as its reliance on military spending. Many families experience food insecurity, which can result in undernutrition, disease, and even death for the children.

The high rates of migration from Eritrea are another indication of the nation's people's suffering and anguish. In quest of safety and a better life, thousands of Eritreans have fled the nation, risking their lives on perilous trips over the sea and desert. Many have passed away or disappeared, leaving their families in an unending state of sorrow and dread. Even those who succeed in getting there frequently still must deal with discrimination, exploitation, and loneliness.

The suffering and sadness of the Eritrean people are also seen in their shared past. The nation has seen a protracted and challenging history of colonialism, conflict, and emigration. Because of the trauma, loss, and relocation that many Eritreans have gone through because of these historical occurrences, there has been generational agony and sadness.

The Eritrean people's suffering and anguish are seen in every area of their life. Much pain and misery have resulted from the government's repressive policies and actions, especially for the nation's youth. The Eritrean people experience agony and sadness because of compulsory military conscription, the incarceration of dissidents, lack of information access, poverty and starvation, and high migration rates. The international community must act immediately to condemn the Eritrean government for its atrocities against humanity and to help the country's citizens.

Both inside and outside of Eritrea, individuals are affected by the nation's agony and loss. Due to the difficult conditions and lack of fundamental freedoms, Eritreans are dispersed around the world as refugees. With loved ones gone missing, held captive, or slain, many families have been shattered. Daily reminders of the human cost of authoritarian governance come from the continued misery and persecution of the Eritrean people.

The issue of the "disappeared," those who have been unlawfully arrested or taken by government authorities and whose whereabouts are unknown, is one illustration of this enduring sorrow and sadness. Their families sometimes spend years looking for them while receiving few to no updates about the whereabouts or health of their loved ones. Many are allegedly being mistreated or imprisoned in secret detention centres, with little chance of release or relief.

Many Eritreans have been driven from their homes because of political persecution, military conscription, or economic hardship in addition to the missing. These people frequently travel on hazardous routes to look for refuge in other nations, and many of them have experienced exploitation, abuse, and violence along the way. The anguish of relocation and the ongoing worry about the welfare of loved ones left behind may be overpowering, even for those who are lucky enough to reach safety.

The accounts of individuals who have managed to flee the nation and find sanctuary elsewhere also show the suffering and sadness of the Eritrean people. The mental and physical scars of torture, incarceration and other types of maltreatment are carried by many Eritrean exiles. Their capacity to start new lives and develop relationships of trust with other people might be negatively impacted by the trauma of their experiences for years or even decades.

The sense of loneliness and helplessness that many Eritreans experience further exacerbates their agony and sadness. Eritreans find it challenging to communicate with one another and acquire reliable news and information about their nation due to the government's severe controls over information and communication. Those who are in exile, who could feel cut off from their cultural and social origins, may experience this sensation of isolation in particular sharpness.

Many Eritreans still put forth a lot of effort to fight for their people's rights and dignity in the face of these obstacles. To bring attention to the ongoing human rights crises in Eritrea, activists, and human rights groups both inside and outside the nation have been recording the wrongdoings carried out by the government. Even while change has been gradual, there have been some encouraging signals, such as a recent peace accord with Ethiopia's neighbour and the release of certain political prisoners. To address the underlying reasons for the suffering and sadness that the Eritrean people continue to endure, however, considerable work still needs to be done.

Both persons within and outside of Eritrea experience the anguish and sadness of the country's citizens regularly. The Eritrean people have suffered from persistent human rights violations, military conscription, economic hardship, and political persecution, which has resulted in relocation, trauma, a feeling of isolation, and impotence. Notwithstanding these obstacles, many people and groups are striving to spread the word about the situation in Eritrea and to fight for the rights and dignity of its citizens. The international community must continue to support these initiatives even if success may be sluggish to make a real difference for the Eritrean people.

Senait's (name changed for privacy) experience of being estranged from her family during the Eritrean independence struggle is one actual instance of the suffering and sadness endured by Eritreans. Senait was only a little child when the war started, forcing her family to leave their home. Senait was cut off from her family during the upheaval of the war and forced to fend for herself.

Senait struggled to survive for years in a refugee camp in Sudan, but she never gave up hope of finding her family again. She had to put up with severe circumstances like intense heat, scarcity of food and water, and the ongoing fear of violence. Senait persevered in the face of these obstacles and finally found her way to the United States, where she was given refuge.

Senait has never really recovered from the trauma of being cut off from her family, though. The fact that she still does not know what happened to her parents or siblings makes her feel quite anxious. Senait has been looking for her family for years but in vain. Even though she works to establish a new life for herself in a foreign nation, she still laments the loss of her family and the life she once knew.

Senait's tale is only one instance of the suffering and loss that many Eritreans have endured because of conflict, displacement, and political repression. The Eritrean people still bear the scars of the independence struggle and the ongoing war with

Ethiopia, and their suffering has only been made worse by the government's oppressive laws and violations of human rights. For many Eritreans, both inside and outside of the nation, the fight for fundamental liberties and the ability to live without intimidation and repression continues.

The life of a guy by the name of Hanibal is an additional illustration of the suffering and anguish endured by Eritreans (name changed for privacy). Hanibal was a university student when the Eritrean government detained him and imprisoned him due to his political convictions. He was detained without contact with his family or a lawyer for months. He endured beatings from his interrogators, forced standing for extended periods, sleep deprivation, and other sorts of abuse throughout this time.

Hanibal was eventually put on trial and accused of crimes against the state. Despite the paucity of evidence against him, he was found guilty and given a life sentence. He was taken to a segregated prison camp where he was subjected to severe living conditions and forced work. Hanibal was forbidden from receiving visits, and his family was unaware of his whereabouts or what had transpired.

Hanibal's loneliness and melancholy grew with time. He battled anxiety and sadness, and his physical condition started to decline. He was refused access to medical treatment and had to live in filthy, cramped circumstances. Despite this, he persisted in fighting for his freedom and never lost hope. Hanibal was freed after years in prison, but his ordeal left an impression on him. He struggled to reintegrate into society after being released from prison because of post-traumatic stress disorder. Also, he endured prejudice and stigmatization from neighbours who perceived him as a criminal.

In Eritrea, thousands of individuals have been tortured, imprisoned, and subjected to various sorts of abuse because of their political convictions. Hanibal's tale is not unusual. Both people who have been imprisoned and their families go through severe and protracted sorrow and loss. A person's mental and physical health may be permanently impacted by the trauma of incarceration and torture, and the stigma of being classified as a criminal may make it much more difficult.

The tale of a family that lost their kid due to the indefinite military duty that is required of all Eritreans is another illustration of the suffering and loss endured by the people of Eritrea. The family only had one kid, who was an intelligent and aspirational young man who wanted to attend college and become a doctor. He was compelled to enlist in the military at age 18 and serve an unlimited amount of time, though. The family was heartbroken since they knew their son's hopes for a better life and a higher education would never come true. Also, they were aware that their son would be exposed to the difficult and sometimes deadly circumstances of military duty, which include little pay, subpar housing, and few opportunities for promotion.

The family got occasional information from their son over time since he was unable to frequently contact them or leave his military camp. They had heard tales of harsh weather exposure, long hours of hard labour, and a dearth of medical care. They discovered that their kid had seen other soldiers receiving severe penalties for small offenses, including beatings, and being made to endure extended periods of exposure to the sun.

The family was devastated to learn that their son had passed away while serving in the military after several years. Little information was given to them about what had happened to him, but they were certain that their worst fears had been realized. Their son's death created a significant and long-lasting void in their family, and they were left to mourn him without any solace or explanation.

This incident is only one of the numerous instances of the suffering and anguish endured by Eritrean families who have lost loved ones to the country's conscription into the military. In addition to denying young people their freedom and opportunity, forced conscription places them in danger and exposes them to physical and psychological torture. Families of these young people must continue to cope with the anguish of learning that their loved ones have perished or are in pain while serving a government that has no regard for human life or personal freedom.

In general, the experiences of individuals like Senait and Hanibal show the profound and continuous suffering and anguish endured by the Eritrean people. Millions of Eritreans have been severely affected by the government's persecution and violations of their human rights, leaving them with severe wounds and trauma that will take centuries to heal. Despite this, the Eritrean people are tenacious and persistent in their quest for their fundamental human rights and freedoms.

Chapter 12
Peace

Peace, justice, and freedom of speech are fundamental values that are essential for a functioning and healthy society. These values are interdependent, and the absence of any one of them can have far-reaching consequences for individuals and communities.

Peace is the foundation of a stable and prosperous society. Without peace, there can be no security, and the lives and livelihoods of individuals and communities are at risk. When conflict arises, it can result in the displacement of people, destruction of homes and infrastructure, and loss of life. In addition to the physical toll of conflict, it can also have long-lasting psychological effects on individuals and communities. The absence of peace can hinder economic growth and development, further exacerbating poverty and inequality.

Justice is essential for ensuring that individuals and communities are treated fairly and that their basic human rights are protected. In a just society, individuals have access to a fair legal system that ensures their rights are protected, and that perpetrators of crimes are held accountable. Justice is crucial for building trust between citizens and their government, and it can help to prevent conflicts and disputes from escalating into violence.

Freedom of speech is also critical for building a healthy and functioning society. It allows individuals to express their opinions and ideas, and to engage in constructive dialogue with others. Freedom of speech is essential for holding those in power accountable, and for promoting transparency and openness in government. It also allows for the free exchange of ideas and knowledge, which can drive innovation and progress.

When peace, justice, and freedom of speech are absent, the consequences can be devastating. Without peace, conflict and violence can ravage communities, leaving a legacy of trauma and destruction. In the absence of justice, human rights abuses can go unchecked, and perpetrators of crimes can act with impunity. And when freedom of speech is curtailed, the voices of the people are silenced, leaving little room for meaningful dialogue and progress.

The importance of peace, justice, and freedom of speech can be seen in the struggles of many countries and communities around the world. In countries where these values are absent, individuals and communities often face significant challenges, including poverty, inequality, and oppression. The absence of these values can lead to the erosion of social trust and the breakdown of social institutions, creating a cycle of violence and instability.

It is essential for governments to prioritize the promotion and protection of these values to ensure the long-term stability and prosperity of their societies. Governments must work to build a legal system that is fair and just, and that provides access to justice for all citizens. They must also ensure that freedom of speech is protected and that individuals have the right to express their opinions and ideas without fear of retribution.

Civil society also plays a crucial role in promoting and protecting these values. Civil society organizations can hold governments accountable for their actions, advocate for the rights of marginalized communities, and promote constructive dialogue and debate. When civil society organizations are free to operate and express their opinions, they can act as a check on the power of governments and other institutions, ensuring that the voices of the people are heard.

In conclusion, peace, justice, and freedom of speech are essential values that are critical for building a healthy and functioning society. When these values are absent, individuals and communities are at risk, and the long-term stability and prosperity of societies are threatened. Governments and civil society organizations must work together to promote and protect these values, ensuring that individuals have access to justice, can express their opinions freely, and live in peace and security. By prioritizing these values, we can create a brighter and more just future for all.

Chapter 13
History and Sea

Eritrea is situated on the Red Sea coast and has a 1,100 km long coastline. A crucial body of water, the Red Sea serves as a commercial and maritime route connecting Asia, the Middle East, and Africa. Eritrea might be a significant participant in the maritime and trade sector due to its location on the Red Sea.

The Eritrean administration has been charged with exploiting the sea for its gain at the expense of the Eritrean people.

The Eritrean government has been charged with leveraging the nation's advantageous Red Sea position to fund terrorist organizations in the area. The Houthi rebels in Yemen, who are involved in a protracted struggle with the Yemeni government, have been charged with being supported by the government. Many people in the international world continue to be dubious despite the Eritrean government's denial of these accusations.

The Eritrean government has also been accused of aiding terrorist organizations and ignoring the needs of the Eritrean people by leveraging its dominance over the Red Sea to boost its economy. Fishing in the Red Sea is now subject to severe government restrictions, which have a catastrophic effect on Eritrea's fishing economy. The government has put severe limitations on the number of fish that may be taken, and Eritrean fishers are prohibited from fishing in some parts of the sea. Due to these restrictions, fewer fish have been caught, which has had a substantial effect on the regional economy.

Human trafficking is a problem that is connected to the exploitation of the sea. Several Eritreans who were carried over the sea to adjacent countries have perished or suffered as a result. Eritreans are among the people who are most susceptible to human trafficking. Many Eritreans continue to risk their lives by crossing the sea in quest of a better life, even though the Eritrean government has done nothing to address this problem.

Calls for the Eritrean government to act to address these problems have grown in recent years. The government has been encouraged by the international community to take action to safeguard its citizens, uphold human rights, and promote sustainable development. Others have urged that the government collaborate with the surrounding nations to create a regional framework for the Red Sea's sustainable management.

The Eritrean government has been hesitant to act despite these demands. Regarding human rights, the administration has a dismal record of accomplishment and has been charged with authoritarianism and repression. The administration has come under fire for being opaque and for refusing to interact with the outside world. As a result, many Eritreans continue to experience the negative impacts of marine resource mismanagement, and the nation's potential to play a significant role in the shipping and commerce industries is still unrealized.

History

Eritrea's struggle to govern its seashore and waterways has a protracted and convoluted history. The different areas that make up modern-day Eritrea, particularly the coastal areas, were ruled by several indigenous kingdoms and sultanates before colonization by Italy.

The coastline and waterways of Eritrea were aggressively exploited for military and economic interests when Italy invaded the country in the late 19th century. Italian and British forces engaged in fierce combat along the shoreline and the surrounding waterways during World War II.

The coastline and waterways were kept under British rule after the war, and Eritrea was given military administration by the British. The authority of the coastline and waterways would thereafter transfer from British to Ethiopian hands when the United Nations General Assembly approved a resolution in 1952 to federate Eritrea with Ethiopia.

Eritreans opposed this choice because they believed it violated their right to self-determination. Early in the 1960s, the Eritrean Liberation Front (ELF) was established to fight for Eritrea's independence and sovereignty over its seas and coastline. A series of military conflicts between the ELF and Ethiopian forces began, and they persisted until Eritrea proclaimed its independence in 1993.

Control over Eritrea's coastline and waterways, however, continued to be a sensitive subject long after independence. According to the UNCLOS, coastal governments have exclusive rights to exploit and manage the natural resources in the waters within a 200-nautical mile Exclusive Economic Zone (EEZ) that extends from their coastline.

Fish are abundant in Eritrea's Exclusive Economic Zone (EEZ), which may also include other resources like oil and gas that are valuable to the nation's economic growth. Nonetheless, disagreements over marine boundaries and fishing rights have arisen because of neighbouring nations, especially Yemen and Saudi Arabia, claiming portions of Eritrea's EEZ as their own.

The Eritrean government has furthermore been charged with damaging the environment and the way its citizens live by overusing its coastline and seas. For instance, despite worries about the possible harm to marine ecosystems and the effect on residents, the government has given foreign businesses permission to engage in offshore mining.

Moreover, Eritrea has been charged with diverting fishing sector profits to the military rather than sustainable management strategies or indigenous fisherfolk. As a result, fish populations have decreased, which has made it more challenging for Eritreans who depend on fishing to make a living.

Notwithstanding these difficulties, various initiatives have been made to encourage sustainable management of Eritrea's seas and shoreline. For instance, the government has collaborated with international groups to develop regulations to combat overfishing and other environmental issues. It has also formed agreements with neighbouring nations to define marine borders.

To manage Eritrea's coastline and waterways in a way that benefits the populace and protects the marine ecology for future generations, however, much more must be done. In addition to resolving the historical and current political and economic issues that have led to the exploitation of this essential resource, this will require a commitment to openness, effective governance, and sustainable management techniques.

Since both nations were under the Italian colonial administration, there has been a long-standing competition between Ethiopia and Eritrea over access to the sea. Ethiopia was given access to the port of Assab, which is situated on the coast of what is now Eritrea, by the United Nations following World War II.

The question of access to the sea became even more crucial after Eritrea declared its independence from Ethiopia in 1993 since it became a landlocked nation without a direct route to the sea. When ties between the two nations worsened and a border conflict broke out in 1998, Ethiopia continued to use the port of Assab for its trade. Tens of thousands of people died because of the two-year battle between Ethiopia and Eritrea. An international panel defined the disputed boundary sections in 2002, although tensions between the two nations still exist.

Since then, Eritrea has constructed its port infrastructure at the port city of Massawa, while Ethiopia still uses the port of Assab as its primary seaport. Yet in recent years, the two nations have moved closer together. A peace agreement was struck in 2018, and since then, border crossings have opened, and diplomatic ties have resumed.

Despite various encouraging improvements, both Ethiopia and Eritrea continue to place a high priority on the problem of sea access. The sea gives essential access to major commerce routes, and having control of significant ports may be advantageous strategically. Likewise, both nations' fishing sectors rely significantly on the ocean.

In general, the competition between Ethiopia and Eritrea for sea access has been a controversial subject for many years, with disputes and tensions resulting from the opposing claims of both nations. Although recent events have raised some optimism for a peaceful ending, it is still unclear how this matter will be settled in the end.

It is impossible to stress how crucial access to the sea is to Eritrea. The nation is strongly dependent on its fishing sector, and the ocean serves as a crucial conduit for international commerce. Moreover, Eritrea has attempted to grow its tourist sector, and having access to the sea is a crucial part of this endeavour.

The exploitation of Eritrea's shoreline, however, is a rising worry. The nation's maritime ecosystem has suffered from overfishing by foreign boats, pollution, and resource extraction by foreign businesses. The absence of regulation and law enforcement in the area exacerbates these problems.

Additionally, the Eritrean government is said to have engaged in unlawful fishing methods that have affected local fishermen's livelihoods and caused a drop in fish populations. In addition, the government has been charged with deploying forced labour on fishing boats, which has resulted in several violations of human rights.

Conflicts with Eritrea's neighbours, notably Djibouti, have also arisen because of the exploitation of its coastline. The two nations fought a brief border conflict in 2008 over a disputed border region that featured sea access. Although the African Union's intervention helped to end the conflict, there is still a lot of animosity between the two nations.

Additionally, the Eritrean government is said to have engaged in unlawful fishing methods that have affected local fishermen's livelihoods and caused a drop in fish populations. In addition, the government has been charged with deploying forced labour on fishing boats, which has resulted in several violations of human rights.

Conflicts with Eritrea's neighbours, notably Djibouti, have also arisen because of the exploitation of its coastline. The two nations fought a brief border conflict in 2008 over a disputed border region that featured sea access. Although the African Union's intervention helped to end the conflict, there is still a lot of animosity between the two nations. The

A variety of economic, social, and environmental variables are all involved in the exploitation of Eritrea's shoreline, which is a complicated problem. The

Eritrean government has made some efforts to solve the problem, but more must be done to guarantee that the nation's maritime resources are safeguarded and maintained sustainably. Also, to solve the larger issue of marine security in the region, coordination and engagement with surrounding nations will be crucial.

Chapter 14
Religion and Choice

The United States Commission on International Religious Freedom (USCIRF) and other groups have ranked Eritrea as one of the world's worst abusers of religious freedom, despite the country's multi-ethnic and multi-religious makeup.

The Eritrean government, led by President Isaias Afwerki, has been accused of pursuing a policy of religious intolerance that aims to restrict and repress religious expression, especially that which it perceives as a challenge to its power. This has shown itself in a variety of ways, including the criminalization of certain religious acts, the intimidation and arrest of religious leaders, and the destruction of houses of worship.

The government's rigorous registration requirements for religious organisations are one of the most critical difficulties affecting religious communities in Eritrea. All religious organisations must register with the government to lawfully function in the country. Yet, the government has made it exceedingly difficult for certain organisations to register, using this to restrict and stifle their activities. Several religious organisations have been awaiting registration for a decade, while others have been denied registration entirely.

The Eritrean government has also curtailed religious liberty through the tight regulation of religious rites. Some religious practises, such as public prayer and preaching, have been prohibited by the government because they pose a danger to its authority. This has resulted in the shutdown of churches, mosques, and other houses of worship, as well as the persecution and imprisonment of religious leaders.

Religious figures have been among the government's primary targets. Some have been held incommunicado for years, while others have been incarcerated without charge or trial. The government has targeted religious leaders for a variety of reasons, including advocating against government programmes and expressing political ideas that the government perceives as a danger.

The incarceration of Patriarch Abune Antonios, the leader of the Eritrean Orthodox Church, is one of the most publicised examples of religious persecution in Eritrea. In 2007, the government removed Patriarch Antonios, who has been under house arrest since. The government accused him of interfering in politics and sowing discord within the church, but many feel his dismissal was motivated by politics.

The Eritrean government has also been accused of targeting religious communities with its national service programme. Both male and female inhabitants of Eritrea are expected to serve in the military for at least 18 months. However, certain religious organisations, such as Jehovah's Witnesses and Pentecostals, have declined to engage in the programme based on their religious beliefs. This has resulted in the arrest and incarceration of members of these groups, who are frequently tortured and mistreated in captivity.

In addition to these direct efforts, the Eritrean government has fostered an atmosphere of fear and intimidation, making it impossible for religious congregations to function freely. Government control of the media and restrictions on information access make it difficult for religious organisations to interact with one another and the outside world. In addition to using informants to monitor religious activities, the government fosters an atmosphere of mistrust and suspicion.

In conclusion, the government of Eritrea's policy of religious intolerance and repression has produced an environment of fear and intimidation for the country's religious communities. The government has infringed the right to freedom of religion in several ways, including through the tight registration procedure, the prohibition of specific religious acts, the targeting of religious leaders, and the use of national service to target religious groups.

Examples

Patriarch Abune Antonios: In 2007, the Eritrean government ousted and placed under house arrest Patriarch Abune Antonios, the head of the Eritrean Orthodox Church. Many feel that his expulsion was politically motivated, even though the government accused him of engaging in politics and separating the church. Since then, he has been held without trial and unable to fulfil his religious obligations.

The Eritrean government has jailed and imprisoned many religious leaders without formal accusation or trial. For instance, the government imprisoned the previous leader of the Eritrean Orthodox Church, Abune Dioskoros, in 2006 and has not released him since. Similarly, the authorities detained other leaders of the Full Gospel Church in 2017, including Pastor Haile Naizghi, who has been imprisoned incommunicado since his detention.

Some religious activities that the Eritrean government deems a danger to its power have been prohibited. For instance, the government has forbidden public prayer and preaching and has shut down many churches and mosques. The government has also prohibited Christians from having marriages and burials in their churches.

National service: Eritrea mandates that all people participate in national duty, which can extend indefinitely. Nonetheless, the government has targeted religious minority who resist national service for religious reasons. Jehovah's Witnesses and Pentecostals, for instance, have been jailed and incarcerated for refusing to serve in the military.

Harassment of religious communities: The Eritrean government has created an atmosphere of fear and intimidation by using informants to monitor religious activities. Members of religious congregations have complained that government agents have followed, harassed, and intimidated them. In addition, the government has restricted information and media access, making it impossible for religious communities to connect with one another and the outside world.

These are only a few instances in which the Eritrean government has infringed the right to religious freedom. The government's policies and actions have fostered an atmosphere of fear and intimidation, making it impossible for religious communities to practise their beliefs freely and publicly.

Chapter 15
Why do Eritreans not defend themselves?

The Eritrean government is notorious for its use of incarceration, torture, and other types of repression to eliminate political opposition and dissent. In 2001, for instance, the government detained several important politicians, journalists, and civil society activists who had advocated for democratic reforms. They were kept without trial and incommunicado for years, and many were tortured and subjected to various sorts of abuse. These activities create an atmosphere of fear and intimidation that makes it impossible for Eritreans to speak out or organise.

Limited Freedom of Speech and Association: The Eritrean government strictly regulates the dissemination of information and the individuals who are permitted to express themselves. In 2009, for instance, the government prohibited all commercial media outlets, leaving only state-controlled media. In addition, the government has outlawed all independent civil society groups, thus restricting the capacity of individuals to organise and advocate for their rights.

Eritrea is one of the poorest nations in the world, with significant rates of unemployment and poverty. The government offers many Eritreans access to basic services and support. This economic dependency can make it difficult for individuals to take risks and advocate for their rights, since they may fear losing their sole source of support.

Divisions & Fragmentation: Eritrea is a country with a great deal of ethnic and linguistic diversity. Historically, these groups have had complicated ties with one another and have occasionally been pitted against one another by the government. During the Eritrean-Ethiopian War in the late 1990s, for instance, the government employed nationalist rhetoric to garner support, frequently at the expense of other communities. This fragmentation might make it challenging for individuals to unite and work towards common goals.

Lack of External Support: The international world has been reluctant to respond to the human rights crisis in Eritrea and has not given civil society groups and activists with sufficient assistance. Several Eritreans who escaped the country and sought safety in other nations were denied refugee status and returned to Eritrea, where they suffer incarceration and torture. This lack of external assistance might make it difficult for Eritreans to affect change on their own and leave them with a sense of isolation and abandonment.

These real-world instances illustrate the numerous obstacles faced by Eritreans who wish to fight for their rights and stand up for themselves. The situation in Eritrea is complex, and the international community must make a coordinated effort to help Eritreans in their fight for human rights and dignity.

Why don't they eliminate him?

Since the country obtained independence from Ethiopia in 1993, the Eritrean government has been in power. The administration, led by President Isaias Afwerki, has been accused of human rights violations, including as limitations on the freedoms of expression, assembly, and religion, as well as the arbitrary arrest and torture of political prisoners.

Over the years, opposition to the government has taken several forms. Early in the twenty-first century, a coalition of politicians, journalists, and civil society activists called for democratic changes and more government accountability by forming the G-15 movement. International outcry resulted from the government's decision to arrest and hold these individuals without trial.

Since then, there have been periodic attempts from within and outside the nation to challenge the regime. Some of these efforts were violent, while others were nonviolent. Here are few instances:

In 1998, Eritrea and its neighbour Ethiopia went to war over a disputed border region. The fight lasted two years and claimed the lives of tens of thousands of individuals. Many viewed the battle as a tactic for the government to divert attention from domestic discontent and mobilise support for a shared cause.

In 2013, a handful of soldiers in Asmara, the capital of Eritrea, launched a mutiny. The insurrection was swiftly suppressed, and all participants were caught and incarcerated.

In 2017, a gang of soldiers attempted to overthrow the government and murder President Isaias Afwerki. The plan failed, and in response, the government launched a crackdown on political dissidents.

Notwithstanding the risks, some Eritreans have engaged in peaceful rallies and civil disobedience to express their discontent. In 2017, for instance, a group of women held a sit-in protest in front of the Ministry of Information in Asmara, requesting information on their incarcerated family members. The demonstration was suppressed rapidly, and the ladies were detained.

Notwithstanding these efforts, the government of Eritrea remains firmly in control. The government controls all elements of public life and has a robust security infrastructure, making it difficult for opposition parties to acquire traction. The government also benefits from the nation's economic reliance on the ruling party, which controls the nation's resources and access to foreign help.

However, the Eritrean government has been effective in silencing critical voices both domestically and internationally. The government has a long history of harassing and intimidating Eritrean dissidents within the nation and in the diaspora who speak out against the government. This has fostered an atmosphere of fear and intimidation, making it hard for alternative organisations to organise and mobilise.

In conclusion, attempts to oppose the Eritrean administration have been ineffective. It has been difficult for opposition parties to acquire traction due to the government's robust security system, control over public life, and economic dependency on the governing party. In addition, the government's brutal handling of dissident voices has fostered an atmosphere of fear and intimidation, making it challenging for opposition organisations to organise and mobilise.

Chapter 16
Lack of Determination

The absence of a constitution can has detrimental effects on a nation and its citizens. A constitution establishes the fundamental ideas and norms that govern how a government runs and interacts with its inhabitants. A government without a constitution may lack legitimacy and be susceptible to corruption and abuse of power. This answer will examine the probable repercussions of a lack of constitution.

Constitutions offer the legal foundation for the preservation of individual rights and liberties. It provides the limitations within which the government can act and outlines the fundamental rights to which citizens are entitled. Without a constitution, citizens are susceptible to abuse at the hands of those in authority. This can result in a lack of faith in government institutions and widespread violations of human rights.

In the lack of a constitution, the power of the government may be ambiguous or challenged, resulting in instability and confusion. This may cause political instability, social discontent, and economic instability. Without defined standards for governance and decision-making, government officials may behave in their own self-interest rather than in the nation's and its citizens' best interests.

Absence of accountability and transparency the constitution offers a foundation for government accountability and openness. It creates processes for holding government officials responsible for their acts and assuring the public's access to information about government activities. There may be no clear processes for maintaining transparency and accountability in the absence of a constitution, which can lead to corruption, abuse of authority, and a decline in public confidence in government institutions.

A constitution gives a framework for resolving essential concerns, such as economic development, social welfare, and environmental preservation. Without a constitution, a government may lack the powers necessary to address these concerns effectively and comprehensively. This may result in economic stagnation, social discontent, and environmental deterioration.

Constitutions give a legal foundation for a government's connections with other nations, making it difficult to establish foreign relations. Without a constitution, a government may find it difficult to create and sustain partnerships with other nations, including commercial deals, diplomatic contacts, and alliances. This can have detrimental effects on a nation's economic and political stability, as well as its capacity to confront global crises.

Absence of legitimacy: A government's legitimacy is founded on its constitution. A government may lack legitimacy in the eyes of its citizens and the international world if it lacks a constitution. This can lead to widespread dissatisfaction with government institutions, a loss of public confidence, and even challenges to the government's authority.

In conclusion, the absence of a constitution can has detrimental effects on a nation and its citizens. It can result in a lack of protection for people' rights, political instability and unpredictability, a lack of openness and accountability, an inability to handle crucial issues, trouble establishing international relations, and a lack of legitimacy. A constitution serves as the basis for the legitimacy of a government by providing a legal framework for governance and decision-making. Thus, it is crucial for a nation to have a well-written and recognised constitution that lays out the fundamental ideas and regulations that govern how the government functions and interacts with its inhabitants.

In Eritrea

Eritrea and its people have been severely harmed by the absence of a constitution. Eritrea, which is in the Horn of Africa, has been governed by the same president, Isaias Afwerki, since achieving independence from Ethiopia in 1993. Since then, there has been no official constitution in the nation, and the president has kept his grip on power by harsh policies and a lack of political and civil rights.

Eritrea's human rights record has been heavily condemned for its failure to defend citizens' rights. Citizens lack a legal foundation for the protection of their individual rights and freedoms due to the absence of a constitution. There have been reports of arbitrary arrests, torture, and forced labour, among other violations of human rights. The administration has also cracked down on freedom of speech, often arresting and detaining journalists, and activists without trial.

Instability and uncertainty: Eritrea's lack of a constitution has contributed to political instability and uncertainty. The government's authority is ambiguous, but the president's authority is absolute. There are no official restraints on his power, and he has demonstrated a readiness to use violence to keep his position. It has conflicted with its neighbours, especially Ethiopia and Djibouti, and its connections with other nations in the area are fragile.

Absence of a constitution has also contributed to Eritrea's lack of openness and accountability. There are no clear accountability systems for government personnel, and the administration has been accused of extensive corruption. Little information is known about the government's revenue sources and expenditures, making the country's economic status similarly cloaked in obscurity.

Eritrea suffers several significant concerns, such as poverty, food insecurity, and lack of access to healthcare and education. It has been difficult for the administration to handle these concerns comprehensively and effectively due to the absence of a constitution. The country relies heavily on foreign help to supply its residents with basic amenities.

Eritrea's connections with other nations are strained due to the government's harsh tactics and lack of political and civil rights. It has been sanctioned by the United Nations and accused of aiding armed organisations in neighbouring nations. This has hindered Eritrea's capacity to create and sustain partnerships with other nations, which has had detrimental effects on its economic and political stability.

Absence of legitimacy: The absence of a constitution has deprived the Eritrean government of legitimacy. The legitimacy of President Afwerki's hold on power is widely questioned, and his administration is frequently referred to a dictatorship. The absence of political and civil rights has also damaged public faith in government institutions, and individuals have had limited opportunity to participate in the administration of their nation.

The absence of a constitution has had enormous detrimental effects for Eritrea and its citizens. Lack of protection for people' rights, political instability and unpredictability, lack of transparency and accountability, failure to handle key issues, difficulty establishing external contacts, and lack of legitimacy have all contributed to the country's continued difficulties. It is imperative that the government of Eritrea establishes a constitution that provides a legal foundation for governance and decision-making and protects the fundamental rights and liberties of its population. Without a constitution, the country would continue to experience political and economic issues and find it difficult to forge connections with other nations in the area and abroad.

Chapter 17
What are the positive aspects?

While Eritrea is frequently in the headlines for its political and socioeconomic issues, it also possesses several good characteristics, such as its rich culture, breath-taking scenery, and strong feeling of community. This essay will explore some of Eritrea's numerous positive attributes.

Eritrea's rich cultural legacy is impacted by its geographical location at the crossroads of Africa, the Middle East, and the Mediterranean. There are nine distinct ethnic groups in the nation, each with its own traditions and customs. There is a significant focus on family, community, and hospitality in Eritrean culture. The nation also has a rich past, with several historic monuments and structures, such as the ancient city of Adulis, which was an important commercial hub in the region surrounding the Red Sea.

Eritrea is a country with breath-taking scenery, from its rocky coastline to its mountains and deserts. The Dahlak Archipelago, a collection of islands in the Red Sea that are home to a diversity of marine species, and the Gash-Barka area are two examples of the country's various ecosystems. There are also several national parks in the country, including Semienawi Bahri National Park and Dankalia Wildlife Sanctuary.

Agriculture and food: Agricultural are a substantial component of the Eritrean economy, employing a considerable section of the people. The country is well-known for its highland-grown coffee and its cattle, goats, and sheep. In addition to being diverse and savoury, Eritrean cuisine places a heavy focus on grains, veggies, and spices. Injera, a sourdough flatbread served with a variety of stews and curries, and zigni, a spicy beef stew, are popular meals.

The country's history of colonialism and commerce, as well as its location at the crossroads of Africa, the Middle East, and the Mediterranean, have shaped its unique culture.

The linguistic variety of Eritrean culture is one of its distinguishing characteristics. The nation has nine officially recognised languages, including the widely spoken Tigrinya, Arabic, and Tigre. Eritrea's complicated past, which includes periods of Italian and Ethiopian occupation, is reflected in the country's linguistic variety.

The culture of Eritrea is also affected by its extensive history of trade and commerce. As a result of the country's long history as a trading hub between Africa, the Middle East, and Europe, its culture reflects a combination of many traditions and practises. The country is recognised for its handicrafts, which include weaving, embroidery, and metalwork, as well as its cuisine, which is influenced by neighbouring countries like as Ethiopia and Sudan.

The music and dancing of Eritrea are also vital to its culture. Instruments such as the krar, a six-stringed lyre, and the Wata, a traditional Eritrean flute, are frequently used to perform traditional Eritrean music, which is renowned for its rhythm and melody. Traditional Eritrean dance is a significant component of the country's cultural history and is frequently performed at festivals and other occasions.

Religion plays an integral part in Eritrean culture. The population is Muslim or Christian, with tiny groups of Jews and Baha'is. Religion has a significant role in daily life, and religious festivals are observed nationwide.

Moreover, family and community are significant parts of Eritrean culture. Elders are widely revered and cherished, and extended families are prevalent in the society. Eritrean culture also places a premium on hospitality, and guests are frequently greeted with warmth and kindness.

Eritrea has worked in recent years to conserve and promote its cultural legacy. Eritrea has developed a variety of cultural institutions and museums, including the National Museum of Eritrea, which highlights the nation's history and cultural heritage. In addition, the government has worked to maintain and preserve its historic buildings and monuments, such as the ancient city of Adulis, which was an important commercial hub in the region.

Eritrea is a country with a rich and diversified culture that has been shaped by its history, geography, and customs. It is a unique and intriguing destination to visit and learn about due to its linguistic and cultural variety, as well as its strong feeling of community and friendliness.

Eritrea is recognised for its rich legacy of handicrafts, including weaving, embroidery, and metalwork. Textiles woven by hand on traditional looms are an especially popular craft in the nation. These fabrics typically include vivid hues and elaborate patterns and motifs.

Eritrea, like many other nations in the area, has a significant tradition of coffee consumption. The coffee ceremony is a significant social and cultural ritual in Eritrea. The ritual includes roasting and brewing coffee, which is then distributed in little cups to the visitors. Guests are often seated around a classic coffee table during the ceremony.

The traditional attire of Eritrea is notable for its brilliant colours and elaborate patterns. Dresses for women are frequently hand-woven and embellished with elaborate embroidery and beads. Typical men's attire consists of a white cotton shirt, pants, and a traditional shawl called a gabi.

The importance of music and dancing in Eritrean culture cannot be overstated. Traditional Eritrean music is distinguished by its rhythm and melody and is frequently performed on instruments like as the krar and the Wata. Traditional Eritrean dance is a significant component of the country's cultural history and is frequently performed at festivals and other occasions.

Eritrean cuisine is inspired by surrounding nations' cuisines, such as Ethiopia and Sudan, as well as the country's trade and commercial history. Typical Eritrean foods include injera (a flatbread prepared from sourdough), tsebhi (a meat and vegetable stew), and shiro (a chickpea stew). Tea and coffee are also widely consumed throughout the nation.

Many significant cultural festivals and festivities are held in Eritrea. The Independence Day ceremony, held on May 24 and commemorating the country's 1991 independence from Ethiopia, is one of the most prominent. Other significant festivals include the Festival of Assumption (a Catholic religious event) and the Festival of Enda Mariam (a commemoration of the country's Orthodox Christian roots).

Why then?

Eritrea's history is an interesting and significant aspect of human history. Even though the country may not always receive the same degree of attention as other nations confronting political and social issues, it is a unique and complicated location with a rich cultural heritage and a fascinating past that is well worth researching. These are a few reasons why understanding about Eritrea's past is crucial, especially in a world where many other nations also face challenges.

Eritrea is primarily a country with a rich and diversified past. From its ancient origins as a commercial centre on the Red Sea to its recent war for independence from Ethiopia, Eritrea's history is filled with interesting tales, momentous events, and prominent personalities. Eritrea knowledge is crucial for anyone who wish to comprehend the larger historical and cultural context of the world in which we live.

In addition, Eritrea is a nation that has suffered severe difficulties in recent years. Despite its hard-won independence in 1991, the country has failed to develop a stable government and economy. As we have noted previously, the present dictatorship in Eritrea is highly criticised for its violations of human rights, and the nation has seen tremendous political instability and economic suffering in recent years. By comprehending Eritrea's past, we may better comprehend the intricate political and socioeconomic aspects that have led to the nation's current difficulties.

Nevertheless, most significant is the reality that Eritrea's past is a tale of endurance and perseverance. The Eritrean people have persisted to strive for their freedom and right to self-determination through centuries of colonisation, tyranny, and conflict. This is a narrative that many people throughout the world are all too acquainted with, and it is profoundly motivating. By studying the history of Eritrea, we may obtain a better understanding of the force of human tenacity and the significance of standing up for what we believe in.

Eritrea is not the only nation facing enormous issues in the globe today. Several nations, like Iran, Ukraine, and others, have their own political, social, and economic difficulties. Nonetheless, this does not lessen the significance of studying Eritrea's history. By investigating the complex difficulties affecting our country, we may obtain a deeper grasp of the larger social, political, and economic factors that are now shaping our globe.

Eritrea's strategic location on the Red Sea is one of its distinguishing characteristics. The nation's history of business and trade dates back thousands of years. Eritrea became a key gateway for commerce between Africa, Asia, and Europe and was home to several mighty dynasties and kingdoms over time. Its extensive history of trade and commerce has left an indelible effect on Eritrea, influencing its culture, people, and economy.

Eritrea's quest for independence is an additional distinguishing characteristic. Eritreans struggled against Ethiopian domination and persecution for decades, culminating in a devastating war that lasted from 1961 to 1991. Despite insurmountable obstacles, the Eritrean people persevered and finally achieved their freedom. This hard-won triumph remains a source of pride and inspiration for the Eritrean people and serves as a vital reminder of the strength of perseverance and will.

Lastly, Eritrea possesses a rich and diversified cultural legacy that merits exploration. Eritrea is a country rich in cultural riches, from its ancient traditions of weaving, metallurgy, and music to its more recent contributions to the worlds of literature and art.

Eritrea's fight for independence was difficult. The nation struggled against Ethiopian sovereignty for thirty years, an arduous and protracted conflict. At this time, many Eritreans were forced to abandon their homes, and the country was left in ruins.

Nonetheless, the Eritrean people's morale never faltered. They continued to struggle for their independence and their rights until they won. This attitude of endurance and tenacity is genuinely unique to Eritrea, and it is something from which the rest of the world may learn.

Eritrea's history is particularly significant since it gives a unique viewpoint on the globe. Eritrea has been disregarded by the world community, and as a result, little is known about its history and culture. But, through studying Eritrea's battle for independence and its distinct culture, we may obtain a greater knowledge of the world and its inhabitants.

In addition, Eritrea's past demonstrates the strength of togetherness. As a result of the people's cohesion, the nation was able to overcome its difficulties and gain independence. This is a strong message that may encourage individuals from all around the world to strive for a shared goal.

In addition, Eritrea's past is significant because it presents a sharp contrast to the media's frequent portrayals. Many Westerners have a mistaken perception of Africa, frequently perceiving it as a continent plagued by poverty, violence, and illness. Yet, Eritrea's history contradicts this narrative by demonstrating that Africa is more complex than the media portrays.

Lastly, Eritrea's history is significant because it is a narrative of hope. The nation has continued to move forward and seek for a better future despite the numerous obstacles it has encountered. This message of hope is vitally needed in the world today, and it is a message that must be shared with everyone.

In conclusion, knowledge of Eritrea's past is essential. It is a tale of tenacity, endurance, solidarity, and optimism. Through studying Eritrea's battle for independence and its distinctive culture, we may obtain a deeper knowledge of the world and its inhabitants. We might also be inspired by the Eritrean people's unyielding spirit and endeavour to create a brighter future for everyone.

Chapter 18
Cycling

Cycling has a long history in Eritrea and is one of the most popular sports in the country. Eritrean cyclists have acquired international attention in recent years, especially for their remarkable achievements in major cycling competitions.

Eritrea has become a cycling superpower in part because of its challenging topography. The nation is situated in the Horn of Africa and is renowned for its rugged and mountainous terrain, making it a wonderful place for cycling. As a result of the fact that many Eritreans grew up using bicycles for transportation, riding has been firmly engrained in the country's culture.

Eritrean cyclists have encountered several obstacles throughout the years. Due to violence and political persecution, many of the country's residents have been compelled to escape its territory. Notwithstanding these obstacles, Eritrean cyclists have persevered to pursue their sport of choice and have become a source of national pride.

Daniel Teklehaimanot is one of the most prominent Eritrean cyclists. He was the first rider from Eritrea to compete in the Tour de France and the first African to wear the King of the Mountains jersey. Also, he has won several other notable cycling competitions, including the Tour of Austria and the Tour of Rwanda.

Merhawi Kudus is an additional renowned Eritrean cyclist. He has also raced in the Tour de France and won several other prestigious competitions, including as the African Continental Road Race Championship.

Besides this, Biniam Girmay is a famous professional cyclist for his climbing skills. Throughout his brief career, he has won the 2018 African Continental Road Race Championship for riders under the age of 23, the 2019 Tour de l'Avenir, and the 2021 African Continental Road Race Championship. On his debut at the 2020 Giro d'Italia, he finished 11th in the general classification despite being the youngest competitor. Biniam's ability and promise have won him distinction as one of the world's best young professional cyclists.

Cycling has also played a significant part in creating national unity in Eritrea. Cycling has facilitated the integration of the country's many ethnic groupings. In truth, the Eritrean national cycling team is comprised of cyclists from many ethnic origins who represent their country on the international arena as a cohesive one.

In recent years, Eritrea has also made substantial expenditures in bicycle infrastructure. The nation has constructed several world-class cycling tracks, notably the Asmara velodrome, one of the greatest in Africa. In addition, the government has provided money for cycling clubs and programmes, which has contributed to the growth of the sport and created possibilities for young people.

In conclusion, riding is an intrinsic part of Eritrean culture, and the country has become a global cycling powerhouse. Despite confronting several obstacles, Eritrean cyclists have persevered in their pursuit of the sport and achieved remarkable success on the world level. Cycling has also played a significant role in fostering national unity and bringing individuals from many ethnic backgrounds together. Eritrea's investment in cycling infrastructure and programmes demonstrates the country's dedication to the sport and its desire to provide its population with possibilities.

Chapter 19
Resources

The mining industry is a major contributor to the country's economy, and some of its minerals are in great demand internationally. Below are some of Eritrea's most abundant natural resources:

Eritrea is believed to contain considerable gold reserves, and gold mining is a significant contributor to the country's economy. A Canadian mining corporation operates the Bisha gold mine, which is in western Eritrea and is one of the country's major mines.

Copper: Eritrea possesses huge copper reserves in the same region as its gold deposits. Copper is utilised in several applications, including electrical wiring and plumbing.

Eritrea is also rich in zinc, which is utilised in a range of sectors, including building, vehicle manufacture, and the fabrication of electrical equipment.

Potash: Eritrea possesses considerable quantities of potash, a vital component of fertiliser. The Colluli potash project, located in eastern Eritrea, is among the world's largest and most sophisticated potash projects.

Eritrea possesses substantial oil and gas deposits, which have not yet been completely explored. The nation is presently investigating chances to expand its oil and gas industry.

In addition to these resources, Eritrea boasts an abundance of animals and a wide variety of flora and fauna. There are various national parks and animal reserves in the country, including Dahlak Marine National Park, which is home to a variety of marine species, including as dolphins, sea turtles, and dugongs. Eritrea is particularly renowned for its historic and distinctive architecture, especially the UNESCO World Heritage-listed structures of Asmara.

Eritrea is a country with an abundance of natural resources, such as gold, copper, zinc, and potash. The mining industry is a significant contribution to the country's gross domestic product, which is highly dependent on it. Eritrea is renowned for its distinctive architecture and diversified animals, which make it an interesting tourist destination.

Despite its abundance of natural resources, Eritrea has had major difficulties in controlling and exploiting them for the benefit of its inhabitants. Lack of openness in the country's mining industry is one of the greatest obstacles. The government has been criticised for its lack of openness and responsibility in managing mining earnings. The Revenue Watch Institute's Resource Governance Index, which examines openness and accountability in the management of natural resources, rated Eritrea lowest in 2013.

In addition, Eritrea has struggled to attract international investment for the development of its natural resources. The political environment and human rights record of the country have discouraged many investors from entering the market, and the government's tight control of the economy has made it challenging for local businesses to succeed. As a result, the advantages of the country's natural riches have not been widely distributed among its population, and many remain impoverished.

Moreover, the exploitation of natural resources has led in environmental damage, particularly in mining-intensive regions. For instance, the Bisha mine has been accused of damaging adjacent water supplies and causing health issues among local inhabitants. The absence of effective environmental legislation and enforcement has let mining firms to operate with disregard for the effects on the environment and surrounding populations.

In addition, the wealth gained from natural resources has not been appropriately spent in social programmes or infrastructure projects that would benefit the country's population. The lack of development and basic amenities, like as healthcare, education, and access to clean water, continues to be a problem for a considerable number of Eritreans.

In conclusion, although Eritrea is rich in natural resources, the lack of management, transparency, and accountability in the country's mining industry, as well as the challenging investment climate, have prevented the advantages of these resources from being evenly distributed among its inhabitants. Moreover, environmental deterioration and a lack of investment in social services and infrastructure have exacerbated these problems.

Chapter 20
Why are Eritreans not prosperous?

Absence of formal education: Many Eritrean refugees are from rural regions with limited access to education or from families unable to afford to send their children to school. In certain rural regions of Eritrea, for instance, families may have no access to schools or must travel considerable distances to attend. This can reduce the educational prospects for young people in these locations.

Eritrean refugees may have endured severe stress and turbulence throughout their lives. Many Eritrean refugees, for instance, have escaped violence or persecution in their own country and may have undergone other traumatic incidents. This might have a lasting effect on their mental health, making it harder for them to concentrate on their professional objectives.

Eritrean refugees may encounter discrimination and prejudice in nations where they seek asylum or resettlement. For instance, they may encounter racism or xenophobia from members of the local community, or they may have difficulty finding job owing to cultural misconceptions or prejudices towards refugees.

In their new countries, Eritrean migrants may lack social networks or contacts that may aid them in navigating the labour market and gaining access to employment possibilities. For instance, they may not have access to mentoring programmes or professional networks that might help them advance their careers.

It may be difficult for Eritrean refugees to have their academic and professional qualifications acknowledged in their new country. For instance, if they acquired their education or training in Eritrea, their credentials in their new nation may not be accepted by companies or educational institutions.

In their new countries, Eritrean refugees may have language obstacles that hinder their ability to communicate effectively, get access to education and training opportunities, and grow in their employment. For instance, to work in their chosen area, they may need to acquire a new language, which can be a big obstacle to success.

Lack of access to resources: Eritrean refugees may not have access to the resources and support services necessary for their professional success. For instance, they may not have access to job training programmes, mentorship opportunities, or financial aid that can aid in the development of their professions. This can restrict their access to the necessary resources and assistance for success.

It is crucial to highlight that these criteria do not apply to all Eritrean migrants and that despite these obstacles, many Eritrean refugees have established successful lives. Nonetheless, these obstacles can be substantial obstacles to success for many refugees, making it more difficult for them to fulfil their career objectives.

Chapter 21
The Prime Minister

Many reasons may contribute to Isaias Afwerki's reputation for being a very secretive individual.

Secondly, as the leader of a nation, he may believe that maintaining a certain amount of privacy is necessary to defend his and the nation's security.

Second, he has a reputation for being extremely careful and calculating in his approach to governing, which may contribute to his reserved personality. He is not renowned for frequently delivering public remarks or doing interviews, and his relations with the media are strictly regulated.

Lastly, reports of human rights violations and other problematic activities by the Eritrean government under the leadership of Isaias Afwerki may discourage him from engaging with the media or openly addressing these concerns.

Isaias Afwerki's private character is due to a variety of circumstances, including his leadership position, his personality and style of governing, and the political context in Eritrea.

Startling truths

The government of Eritrea has been accused of instituting a system of indefinite national service that mandates all people to serve in the military or other government posts for an indeterminate period. Several Eritreans have been recruited against their choice, with others compelled to serve for years.

There have been several instances of inmates in jail in Eritrea being tortured, beaten, and subjected to various sorts of cruelty. Several convicts have been imprisoned without trial or legal counsel for years.

The Eritrean government strongly regulates the media and restricts freedom of expression, especially the ability to criticise the government. Independent journalists have been imprisoned, and many Eritreans fear reprisal if they speak out against the government.

The Eritrean government has been accused of persecuting religious minorities, particularly Christians and Muslims who do not subscribe to the government's favoured interpretations of their respective religions. Some groups' members have been arrested and detained, and their places of worship have been closed.

Never returning

The government's policy of restricting the movement of its residents, which makes it difficult for Eritreans who leave the country to return, is one of the topics that has attracted widespread attention.

This approach has had catastrophic effects on both inside and outside Eritreans.

The policy of restricting Eritreans' freedom of movement dates to 1993, when the country gained its independence. The government of Eritrea enacted a national service programme mandating that all citizens, male and female, serve in the military or civil service for an unspecified amount of time. There is no defined end date for the duration of the service, which may span years. As a result, many young Eritreans are forced into the military or public service and are unable to leave until their duty is complete.

Many Eritreans prefer to leave the nation in quest of better prospects and a better life since the situation has grown so terrible. Nevertheless, as they depart, they are confronted with the fact that they cannot return. Before leaving Eritrea, all nationals are required to get an exit visa from the government. This visa is difficult to get, and people suspected of wishing to leave the country permanently are frequently refused.

Even individuals who successfully secure an exit visa and leave the country are not assured a return. Eritrea's government has enacted a policy requiring all emigrants to pay a 2% tax on their outside earnings. This fee is collected by Eritrean embassies across the world and is viewed as a tool for the government to keep control over its nationals who have emigrated. Failing to pay the tax may result in the refusal of a visa or other punishments.

The policy of limiting Eritreans' freedom of movement has had severe effects on individuals who have fled the nation. Many displaced Eritreans cannot reconcile with their relatives or return to their homes. As a result, many Eritreans are currently living in exile, unable to return to their nation of origin.

The approach has also had a significant effect on the economy of Eritrea. Many Eritreans who have emigrated are highly educated and competent individuals who may contribute to the nation's growth. Yet, the policy of restricting Eritreans' freedom of movement has resulted in a brain drain, with many of the country's brightest and finest departing and never returning. This has had a negative influence on the country's capacity to develop and compete internationally.

The government of Eritrea has been accused of several human rights violations, including the use of forced labour, arbitrary incarceration, and torture, in addition to restricting the mobility of its residents. Many Eritreans who have fled the nation to seek a better life have done so to avoid these injustices.

In conclusion, the policy of restricting Eritreans' freedom of movement has had disastrous effects for Eritreans both inside and outside of the nation. Many Eritreans living in exile are unable to reconcile with their families or return to their homes because Eritreans who have left the nation are unable to return. This legislation has negatively impacted the nation's economy and its capacity to compete internationally. The international community must act to resolve this issue and exert pressure on the Eritrean government to reform its policies and respect its citizens' fundamental human rights.

What is the consequence of this?

The policy of restricting Eritreans' freedom of movement and the difficulty of Eritreans to return to their own country can have a substantial effect on the mental health of individuals affected. The following are probable consequences:

Eritreans who have left the nation and cannot return may feel a tremendous feeling of disconnection from their relatives, friends, and country. This might result in emotions of loss, sadness, and isolation, which can have a detrimental effect on their mental health.

Anxiety and worry: Eritreans who are unable to return to their home country may face anxiety and fear due to the uncertainty of their future, such as not being able to care for ailing family members or return for significant life events. This might result in emotions of powerlessness, despondency, and dread of the unknown.

Trauma and PTSD (Post Traumatic Stress Disorder): Eritreans who have fled their country because of persecution, violence, or conflict may develop trauma-related symptoms like flashbacks, nightmares, and hypervigilance. In addition, they may acquire post-traumatic stress disorder (PTSD), which can have long-term implications on their mental health.

Depression and other mood disorders: Eritreans who are unable to return home may develop depression and other mood disorders because of their sense of loss and estrangement. Moreover, they may suffer pessimism, worthlessness, and a lack of desire.

Eritreans who are unable to return home may feel social isolation and a lack of connections with others. This might be especially difficult for people who fled their nation alone and have little support networks.

Stigma and discrimination: Eritreans unable to return home may face stigma and prejudice in their host nations. This can worsen their mental health symptoms and create further hurdles to receiving treatment.

In conclusion, the policy of restricting Eritreans' freedom of movement and the difficulty of Eritreans to return to their home country might have substantial effects on their mental health. These effects consist of separation and loss, anxiety and dread, trauma and PTSD, depression and other mood disorders, social isolation, stigma, and prejudice. It is essential for the international community to acknowledge these effects and seek to mitigate them, especially by providing mental health care and advocating for Eritreans' fundamental human rights.

Chapter 22
Women's Equality

For many years, the subject of women's rights in Eritrea has been a source of worry. While considerable progress has been made in recent years, Eritrean women continue to confront several obstacles.

Gender-based violence is one of the greatest difficulties. In Eritrea, domestic violence, including physical and sexual abuse, is widespread. The government has passed legislation criminalising such conduct, but implementation and enforcement remain deficient. The continuance of gender-based violence is also aided by cultural norms that promote male dominance and female subjugation.

Women have restricted access to education and career possibilities. Despite the absence of legal discrimination against women in school or work, societal expectations and cultural norms frequently restrict women's chances. This might result in economic dependence and make it challenging for women to express their rights in other areas.

A further obstacle for women in Eritrea is their restricted political participation. Women are underrepresented in positions of political leadership, and women's political engagement is often low owing to a lack of understanding, social stigma, and cultural beliefs.

The Eritrean government has taken attempts to strengthen women's rights in recent years. For instance, it has enacted a national strategy on gender equality and created a ministry charged with advancing women's rights. In addition to expanding women's access to education and healthcare, the government has made initiatives to fight gender-based violence.

Nonetheless, progress has been sluggish, and there is still a great deal of work to be done in Eritrea to promote women's rights. The international community may assist initiatives to promote women's access to education, employment, and political representation in Eritrea and advocate for women's rights.

Examples

Domestic violence is a common issue in Eritrea, with several women facing physical and sexual abuse at the hands of their boyfriends. For instance, a 2014 United Nations investigation indicated that more than half of Eritrean women polled had experienced physical or sexual abuse at the hands of their boyfriends.

While education is mandatory in Eritrea, many girls are unable to attend school because of poverty, cultural views, and the necessity to assist with home tasks. Human Rights Watch reports that more than

60 percent of Eritrean women are illiterate, and that females are more likely to drop out of school than boys.

Eritrean women have limited access to formal work due to several substantial hurdles. For instance, according to a 2017 survey by the World Bank, just 14% of women in Eritrea were working outside of agriculture, while 44% of males were.

In positions of political leadership in Eritrea, women are underrepresented. Currently, there are no women in the Government or National Parliament of Eritrea. Women's political involvement is similarly low, as many women face cultural hurdles that prevent them from participating in politics.

All inhabitants of Eritrea are obligated to do obligatory military duty. Nonetheless, service is frequently indefinite, with many conscripts serving without pay or fundamental rights for years. Women enlisted personnel are especially susceptible to sexual harassment and assault.

These cases illustrate the obstacles Eritrean women face about their rights. Although though there have been some good changes in recent years, such as the formation of a ministry for women's affairs, there is still more work to be done to guarantee that women in Eritrea may enjoy their full human rights.

Chapter 23
People are Brian washed

The split of Eritreans abroad is a complicated and diverse topic with origins in the nation's history, politics, and diaspora populations.

Political disagreements are one of the primary drivers of discord among Eritreans in foreign countries. Since its independence in 1993, Eritrea has been governed by the People's Front for Democracy and Justice (PFDJ). Several Eritrean diaspora communities have condemned the government for its lack of democracy, violations of human rights, and mandatory military service. This has led to a schism between supporters and opponents of the government.

In certain instances, these political disagreements have sparked tensions and even bloodshed within Eritrean expatriate groups. In 2019, for instance, pro-government and anti-government Eritrean protestors clashed in Germany, resulting in injuries and arrests.

Cultural and linguistic disparities among Eritrean diaspora populations are another source of discord. There are nine distinct ethnic groups in Eritrea, each with its own language and culture. These disparities might cause conflicts and misunderstandings between members of various diaspora communities.

Also, Eritrean diaspora communities exhibit generational disparities. Certain elements of Eritrea's history, like as the war for independence, may have been experienced by older generations vs younger generations. This can result in divergent priorities and viewpoints, which can contribute to divisiveness.

Positive aspects of the government

There are several reasons why some Eritreans who have emigrated may still support the government.

Fear of persecutors: Eritrea is a very authoritarian nation with restricted speech and association rights. Speaking out against the government or expressing dissident viewpoints may result in persecution, jail, or worse for Eritreans. Some Eritreans may consequently show support for the government out of concern for their own and their loved ones' safety.

Eritrea is a young nation, having only achieved independence from Ethiopia in 1993. Many Eritreans have a keen sense of nationalism and patriotism, and they may see the government as the genuine representation of the nation and its people. They may also view the government's actions as essential for preserving Eritrea's independence and sovereignty.

Some Eritreans who have left the country may nonetheless have economic and/or social links with the government. For instance, they may have relatives who are government employees or who depend on government services for their living. As a means of safeguarding their loved ones, individuals may declare support for the government under such circumstances.

The Eritrean government has a history of manipulating public opinion and suppressing opposition via the use of propaganda and false information. Eritreans who have left the country may still be exposed to such propaganda via government-controlled media sources or social networks, which may affect their opinions of the government.

It is essential to highlight, however, that not all Eritreans who express support for the government do so for the same reasons, and that many Eritreans criticise the policies and acts of the government. The reasons for supporting or opposing the government are numerous, complicated, and dependent on the individual's experiences, beliefs, and circumstances.

Propaganda

The Eritrean government has been accused of utilising propaganda to sway public opinion and control the narrative. The government has been accused of utilising the following methods:

State-controlled media: The Eritrean government has complete control over the country's media outlets, which are entirely government-owned. This enables the government to control the dissemination of news and information to the public and to censor or suppress any dissenting ideas or opinions.

The Eritrean government has been accused of disseminating incorrect or misleading information to misinform or confuse the populace. For instance, the government has been known to circulate false stories about opposition organisations or foreign countries to install popular fear and distrust.

The Eritrean government has been accused of utilising schools and other educational institutions to indoctrinate pupils and promote official ideology through propaganda efforts. The government has also been accused of utilising propaganda to establish a cult of personality around its leaders, such as former President Isaias Afwerki.

The Eritrean government has been accused of repressing opposition voices and critics via harassment and intimidation. This may involve physical assault, arrest, incarceration, and other types of harassment or persecution.

Many view the Eritrean government's use of propaganda and deception as a means of controlling the narrative and maintaining its hold on power. Yet, these strategies have a negative effect on the country's citizens by restricting their access to information and inhibiting free speech and criticism.

Examples

Many instances exist of the Eritrean government employing propaganda to sway public opinion and stifle opposition. Here are some instances from actual life:

All media outlets in Eritrea are owned and operated by the government, which strictly regulates the dissemination of information to the public. The government owns and operates the country's only newspaper, as well as its only television and radio stations. It is well known that the media censors or suppresses any critical ideas or thoughts.

The Eritrean government has been known to disseminate false or misleading information to misinform or confuse the populace. For instance, in 2019, the government accused the United Nations of attempting to "inundate" Eritrea with refugees to destabilise the stability of the nation. The charge was seen as unfounded and an attempt to shift attention from the government's poor human rights record.

It has been shown that the Eritrean government uses schools and other educational institutions to indoctrinate pupils and promote official ideology. For instance, in 2018, the government created a national service programme for high school students that was widely perceived as a means of indoctrinating youths with government ideology. Students were forced to spend a year in military training and on government projects, such as road construction and tree planting.

Harassment and intimidation: The Eritrean government has a history of using harassment and intimidation to stifle critics and opposition voices. In 2001, for instance, the government imprisoned several lawmakers and journalists who had questioned its human rights record. Several of the so-called "G-15" were tortured or subjected to various sorts of brutality while imprisoned incommunicado for years.

These are only a few instances of how the Eritrean government uses propaganda and disinformation to dominate the narrative and stifle opposition. When they restrict access to information and hinder free speech and criticism, such measures may have a devastating effect on a country's citizens.

Chapter 24
Young Adults

For many years, the treatment of young people in Eritrea has been a source of concern. The country's mandatory and indefinite national service policy, which mandates all able-bodied men and women to serve in the military or other government-controlled sectors for an indeterminate amount of time, has had a substantial effect on the nation's youth.

Following are some examples of how Eritrea treats its youth:

All young people in Eritrea are forced to enrol in a national service programme that might continue for years or even decades. The programme features little pay, terrible living circumstances, and severe treatment, including as physical torture, forced work, and other sorts of mistreatment. Several young individuals are compelled to serve in the military for extended periods of time, often with no end in sight.

The Eritrean government has been accused of restricting education opportunities for the nation's youth. This includes restricting access to higher education for people who do not finish their national service and reducing the number of schools and institutions in the country. Many young people are unable to attend school or seek further education because they are obligated to serve in the military or are in the process of completing their service.

For many years, the treatment of minors in Eritrea has been a source of concern. The country's mandatory and indefinite national service policy, which mandates all able-bodied young men and women to serve in the military or other government-controlled sectors for an undetermined amount of time, has had a substantial effect on the country's younger population.

Following are some examples of how minors are treated in Eritrea:

Youngsters as young as 16 years old are frequently recruited against their will to engage in the national service programme. This is a violation of international human rights law, which forbids the recruitment of minors under 18 into armed forces or groups.

Due to the required national service programme, Eritrean youngsters under the age of 18 have restricted access to schooling. Since they are compelled to serve in the military or other government-controlled industries, numerous young people are unable to attend school or seek further education.

Underage recruits to the national service programme are frequently exposed to physical abuse and forced labour, as well as other types of mistreatments. If they fail to cooperate, they may be beaten, tortured, or subjected to other maltreatment.

Separation from families: young people who are compelled to participate in the national service programme may be isolated from their families for years. This can have a significant effect on their mental health and well-being, as well as their family ties.

These are but a few instances of the manners in which minors are treated in Eritrea. When they limit access to education, subject children to abuse and forced labour, and isolate them from their families, these practises can have a devastating effect on the country's juvenile population.

Chapter 25
Artist

Eritrea's art scene is not well-known internationally, and Eritrean artists have little prospects to achieve worldwide recognition and financial success. Several artists face constraints on their creative expression and restricted possibilities to exhibit their work because of the political and economic climate of the country.

In contrast, artists from several other regions of the globe have greater opportunity to exhibit their work and achieve financial success. There are several galleries, museums, and other cultural organisations that support and promote international artists in major art cities such as New York, Paris, and London. This has led to the rise of many successful artists, including painters, sculptors, photographers, and other creative professions, who are able to make a livelihood from their work.

In addition to financial success chances, artists in other regions of the world frequently have greater freedom of expression and can explore a broader range of creative ideas and styles without fear of political harassment. This can result in more inventive and diversified artistic production, which in turn garners greater worldwide attention from the art community.

In general, the chances and obstacles Eritrean artists face are distinct from those of their colleagues in other countries. There are unquestionably brilliant artists in Eritrea, but the country's political and economic climate restricts their chances of recognition and financial success.

Normalization

Normalization of suffering and agony in Eritrea is a difficult subject strongly rooted in the country's culture and history. Decades of conflict, political persecution, and economic hardship have taken a toll on the physical and emotional health of the country's citizens.

As a result, many Eritreans have become accustomed to pain and suffering as an everyday occurrence. This is especially true for trauma sufferers, including military veterans, political prisoners, and refugees. In many instances, the normalising of misery and pain has become a coping technique that enables individuals to endure in tough situations.

For instance, many Eritreans who are recruited into the country's forced national service programme endure difficult living circumstances, long hours of challenging work, and physical and mental torture. Despite these conditions, many troops stay to serve for years, and some even declare devotion to the administration accountable for their torture.

This phenomenon is not exclusive to the national service programme. Many Eritreans who have departed the country as refugees have endured traumatic experiences throughout their travels and in their new homes. Due to the normality of pain, however, they may be reluctant to seek assistance or share their experiences.

Eritrea's history and political climate have developed a complicated problem including the normalising of misery and agony. It is crucial to understand the impact this normalisation has on individuals and communities, and to give assistance and tools to help people recover from trauma and heal. It is also crucial to address the underlying causes of misery and agony in Eritrea, such as the need for improved political and economic stability and an end to human rights violations.

In addition to being a deeply rooted cultural phenomena, the normalisation of misery and anguish in Eritrea is a violation of basic human rights. In accordance with the International Declaration of Human Rights, everyone has the right to a life free from torture, cruel, inhuman, and degrading treatment, and punishment.

The normalisation of misery and anguish in Eritrea is especially alarming considering the terrible human rights abuses and breaches that have happened in the nation. The Eritrean government has been accused of several violations of human rights, including as arbitrary imprisonment, torture, and extrajudicial murders.

In addition, the acceptance of suffering and grief can prolong a cycle of violence and trauma. As individuals become desensitised to violence and abuse, they may be more inclined to engage in such behaviour themselves. This can result in a difficult-to-break cycle of violence and trauma.

The normalisation of suffering and anguish may also result in a lack of accountability for violations of human rights. When suffering and grief are seen as usual, it might be more challenging to recognise and handle incidents of abuse. This can maintain a culture of impunity for those who violate human rights and make it more difficult for victims to seek justice and reparation.

It is crucial to acknowledge that the normalisation of suffering and anguish in Eritrea is a violation of fundamental human rights, and that tackling this issue needs a comprehensive strategy that targets the main causes of human rights violations in the nation. This includes measures to foster more political and economic stability, stop the practise of mandatory national service, and bring those guilty for human rights violations to justice. It also entails giving survivors of abuse with assistance and resources and striving to alter societal views on suffering and pain.

Chapter 26
We tend to take things for granted

As humans, we frequently take both large and tiny things for granted, failing to recognise their full worth. We think that things will always be the same, and we do not really value what we have until it is no longer accessible. This might result in a lack of gratitude and the inability to fully appreciate the present. Examine a few instances of items that we take for granted daily.

One of the most essential things we take for granted is clean water. Most of us have access to clean water anytime we desire it, but we rarely consider how incredible it is that we can just turn on a faucet to have fresh, drinking water. In many regions of the world, people must travel great distances to obtain water, which is frequently polluted and causes illness and disease.

Another thing we take for granted is electricity. The flip of a switch provides light and electricity. We do not realise how dependent we are on energy until a blackout leaves us in the dark, unable to charge our electronics or cook our food.

Also, we take our health for granted. We assume we will always be healthy and do not take the required precautions to preserve our health. When we become ill, we frequently regret not having taken better care of ourselves. Also, we tend to disregard the effect of our lifestyle choices on our health until it is too late.

Also taken for granted are our interpersonal ties. We do not make the effort to preserve our connections with our loved ones because we believe they will always be there for us. We fail to show our appreciation and affection for people around us, and only when we experience loss or separation do we grasp the actual significance of these connections.

The natural world is also taken for granted. We presume that natural resources will always be accessible, and we do not consider the environmental impact of our actions. We degrade natural ecosystems and contaminate the air and water without contemplating the long-term effects.

In addition to these examples, there are several more things that we take for granted, such as access to education, technology, and the ability to freely express ourselves. We do not recognise the significance of these items until they are unavailable.

Taking things for granted frequently results in a lack of gratitude and appreciation for the present. We become so preoccupied with what we lack that we fail to value what we do have. This might result in emotions of discontent, worry, and sadness.

To avoid taking what we have for granted, it is essential to nurture a sense of thankfulness and appreciation. This may be accomplished by periodically pausing to consider the blessings in our life, expressing gratitude for the people in our lives, and taking care of our health and wellbeing.

By identifying the things, we take for granted and making a concerted effort to appreciate them, we may have richer and more fulfilled lives. Moreover, we may learn to be more conscious and present in the now, which can help us discover joy and satisfaction in even the simplest of things.

Chapter 27
Water and Electrical Power

Access to power and clean water is a fundamental human right, yet many Eritreans lack access to these resources. Eritrea's electrical and water infrastructures are poor, resulting in frequent blackouts and a dearth of clean water for drinking, cooking, and hygiene.

In Eritrea, electricity is a precious resource, and the nation has endured chronic power outages for decades. Several homes and businesses rely on diesel generators for electricity, but these generators are costly to operate and maintain. The inconsistent and costly electricity supply has hampered economic growth and impeded the nation's development.

Access to electricity is even more restricted in rural regions, with many people depending on traditional energy sources such as wood and charcoal. These energy sources are not only harmful to the environment, but also represent a substantial health risk owing to indoor air pollution.

The water situation is similarly severe. Availability to potable water is a significant problem in Eritrea, especially in rural regions. The bulk of the population obtains their daily water supply from wells or water trucks, as the nation has few natural sources of fresh water. Many individuals must travel great distances to acquire water that is frequently polluted and unfit for consumption. This causes extensive health issues, especially among youngsters, who are especially susceptible to waterborne infections.

In Eritrea, the lack of access to clean water and dependable energy has a huge influence on the everyday life of the population. It impacts health, as well as access to education, economic opportunities, and quality of life. Without access to energy, companies cannot function properly, and without clean water, individuals cannot maintain good hygiene or cultivate crops, resulting in food insecurity.

The Eritrean government has been attempting to repair the nation's infrastructure, particularly the water and electrical networks, but progress has been slow owing to a lack of investment and limited resources. Government initiatives to encourage renewable energy sources such as wind and solar power have been sluggish to produce fruit.

In conclusion, the lack of access to power and clean water is a significant problem in rural regions of Eritrea. The condition has a considerable influence on economic and social growth, as well as the health and well-being of individuals. To strengthen the infrastructure and guarantee that everyone has access to these fundamental resources, further investment and resources are required.

Why should I to care?

There are several reasons why people should be interested in Eritrea's history. Eritrea's narrative deserves investigation, from its rich history and culture to its contemporary political and socioeconomic issues.

Secondly, Eritrea is a nation with a rich and varied past. It was an important hub of trade and culture in the ancient world and has been inhabited for aeons by several ethnic groups. It has been a hub of warfare and trade throughout history due to its location along the Red Sea and its strategic importance. Knowing Eritrea's past is essential to comprehending the country's current position and its significance in the region.

Eritrea's present political crisis is another cause to care about the country. Since its independence from

Ethiopia in 1993, Eritrea has been administered by the same government, which has been accused of human rights breaches, including limitations on free expression and political opposition, compulsory conscription, and torture. A considerable number of Eritreans have fled the nation in pursuit of safety and better prospects because of these problems.

The situation of Eritrean refugees is an additional reason people should be interested in Eritrea's history. The country is one of the world's major suppliers of refugees, with thousands of people escaping annually. In quest of safety and better chances, many of these migrants undertake perilous trips, typically over the Sahara Desert and across the Mediterranean Sea. Knowing the reasons why individuals leave Eritrea and the obstacles they confront on their trips is crucial for comprehending the worldwide refugee issue and the need for solutions.

Eritrea's history has broader ramifications for the Horn of Africa and the surrounding area. Eritrea has been involved in several disputes, including a boundary dispute with Ethiopia that led to war in the late 1990s and ongoing problems with other bordering nations. In terms of security and stability, the political situation in Eritrea has also had repercussions on the surrounding region.

The culture and arts of Eritrea offer an additional cause to care about the country. Eritrea has a rich creative and cultural legacy, including influences from

Africa, the Middle East, and Europe. Eritrean music has garnered worldwide popularity, with performers like as the late Abraham Afewerki and the renowned ensemble Wedi Tukul garnering international fame. Knowing and respecting Eritrea's culture is essential for fostering cross-cultural understanding and respect.

Concern for the history of Eritrea is crucial for advancing human rights and dignity. The obstacles experienced by the Eritrean people, such as limits on free expression, conscription, and restricted access to basic resources, violate the ideals of human rights and dignity. To promote a fairer and more equitable world, it is vital to comprehend these obstacles and advocate for their resolution.

There are several reasons why individuals should care about the history of Eritrea. Eritrea's narrative deserves investigation, from its rich history and culture to its contemporary political and socioeconomic issues. By comprehending and interacting with Eritrea's history, we may foster cross-cultural understanding, fight for human rights, and strive towards a fairer and more equitable world.

◆

Chapter 28
Why is nobody willing to speak up?

Eritrea is a small African nation located on the Horn of Africa, and it has experienced several obstacles throughout the years. Despite the numerous issues and injustices, the country has endured, it is frequently neglected by the international world, and few individuals appear to advocate for its rights and interests. Many causes, including political and economic interests, ignorance, and the country's relative isolation, contribute to this situation.

Eritrea has not garnered much attention from the international world due in large part to its strategic position. Eritrea, which borders the Red Sea, is a vital transit point for transportation and commerce between Europe, Asia, and Africa. This has made the nation a target for foreign powers attempting to establish a foothold in the area, as well as a target for external pressures and interventions. For fear of upsetting the delicate balance of power in the area, many nations and international organisations are hesitant to engage in Eritrea's internal affairs.

Another reason Eritrea is frequently disregarded is a lack of awareness and knowledge. Several individuals throughout the globe are unfamiliar with the country, its history, and its current position. This lack of understanding can lead to indifference and inaction, since individuals are more likely to support issues that are known to them and that resonate with their own experiences.

In addition, Eritrea's history of isolationism and self-reliance has led to its low level of participation with the international community. Since its independence in 1993, the nation has been governed by the same administration, which has been accused of human rights violations including limits on free expression and political opposition, compulsory conscription, and torture. Eritreans have fled the country in pursuit of safety and better prospects, further isolating the nation from the rest of the world.

Additionally, the economic predicament of Eritrea might be related to the lack of participation and support for the nation. Eritrea is among the world's poorest nations, having a low GDP and a high unemployment rate. Because of this, many international organisations and governments perceive the country as a liability rather than an advantage. This has made it impossible for Eritrea to get the help and support it needs to thrive and prosper, compounding the country's difficulties and isolation.

Eritrea's internal issues also contribute to the country's lack of international backing. The Eritrean government has a reputation for being autocratic and harsh, with little tolerance for dissent or opposition. As a result, many individuals are afraid to interact with or support the government for fear of appearing complicit in its acts. This has made it challenging for Eritreans to garner support and campaign for their own rights and interests.

Eritrea has not gotten the assistance and attention that it needs from the international community for several reasons. They include political and commercial interests, a lack of knowledge and information, isolationism, economic obstacles, and internal politics. Yet, it is essential to acknowledge the obstacles Eritrea confronts and to work towards fostering more awareness, understanding, and support for the country and its people. By doing so, we may promote more justice, dignity, and prosperity for all people and move towards a more fair and just global community.

Eritrean Government

The Eritrean government has been accused of several violations of human rights, including as limits on free expression and political opposition, forced conscription, and torture. Notwithstanding these charges, the international community has not taken serious action against the administration. Many reasons, including the country's isolation, strategic importance, and lack of political will and resources to hold the administration responsible, contribute to this situation.

Due in large part to the country's relative isolation, the Eritrean leadership has not been held responsible. Eritrea has a tradition of independence and isolationism, and it has been hesitant to participate with the international world. As a result, foreign organisations and governments have found it difficult to monitor the situation in Eritrea and hold the government accountable for its actions.

In addition, Eritrea's government has strategic significance due to its location along the Red Sea. This has made it a target for foreign powers seeking a presence in the area, as well as a target for external pressures and interventions. As a result, many nations and international organisations hesitate to act against the Eritrean government for fear of upsetting the region's delicate balance of power.

Moreover, the Eritrean administration has not been held accountable due to a lack of political will and resources. Several nations and international organisations prioritise economic progress, security, and stability. Thus, they may lack the means and political will to confront human rights violations in Eritrea. In addition, several nations may have economic or geopolitical reasons for keeping good relations with the Eritrean government, making it harder to act against them.

Moreover, the Eritrean administration is good at diverting criticism and portraying itself as a victim of international influence. The administration asserts that allegations of human rights violations are false and part of a bigger effort to undermine the sovereignty and independence of the nation. As a result of creating a narrative of resistance and defiance, this discourse has made it more difficult for the international community to act against the administration.

The difficulty of exposing human rights violations in general may also contribute to Eritrea's government's lack of accountability. Even when human rights violations are documented, it can be challenging to find a mechanism to hold the offenders responsible. This is especially true when the abuses are perpetrated by a government that has the means and authority to suppress opposition and preserve control.

There are assorted reasons why the Eritrean government has not been held accountable for its human rights violations. This includes the country's isolation, its strategic importance, the absence of political will and resources, the government's attitude of resistance, and the difficulties of confronting human rights violations in general. Yet, it is essential to continue advocating for justice and accountability in Eritrea and to support the efforts of Eritreans and international groups fighting towards greater human rights and liberty for the Eritrean people. By doing so, we may promote more justice, dignity, and prosperity for all people and move towards a more fair and just global community.

There are several parallels between Hitler and Isaias Afwerki.

Adolf Hitler, the terrible head of the Nazi party, and Isaias Afwerki, the President of Eritrea, are two incredibly distinct historical characters. Nonetheless, there are significant parallels and variations in their approaches to leadership.

Hitler and Afwerki's attitude to totalitarianism is one of their most significant parallels. Both leaders want complete control over their subjects' lives, including their political views, personal life, and economic possibilities. This is obvious in their implementation of one-party regimes, suppression of political opposition, and employment of propaganda to preserve power.

Both presidents employ military force to attain their aims, which is another commonality between them. World War II was distinguished using military force and horrors such as the Holocaust because of Hitler's expansionist goals. Likewise, Afwerki's administration has been accused of severe violations of human rights, such as the use of compulsory conscription and the repression of political opposition.

There are, nevertheless, significant contrasts between Hitler and Afwerki. The most striking distinction between their ideas is their character. Nazi ideology stressed the supremacy of the Aryan race and the necessity to destroy "inferior" populations such as Jews and Romani people. Afwerki's worldview is founded on a kind of nationalism that stresses Eritrea's independence and sovereignty.

The way the two leaders ascended to power is a second significant distinction between them. Hitler rose to power in Germany through a combination of political intrigue and bloodshed, including the notorious "Night of the Long Knives" in which he exterminated his political opponents. Afwerki, on the other hand, played a pivotal role in the Eritrean independence struggle and became the country's first president once independence was achieved in 1993.

In addition, the two leaders have distinct economic perspectives. Hitler's economic policies stressed expansion and the construction of a war economy, whereas Afwerki's administration has prioritised self-reliance and the growth of the domestic sector. Nonetheless, both presidents have been condemned for their lack of care for the well-being of their population, especially in terms of social welfare programmes and human rights.

The character of the two presidents' legacies is an additional significant distinction between them. Due to the atrocities committed by his administration during World War Two, Hitler is recognised as one of the most wicked and destructive characters in human history. Afwerki is credited with guiding Eritrea to independence, but he has also been condemned for his dictatorial reign and violations of human rights.

There are considerable variations between Hitler and Afwerki in their philosophies, ascent to power, economic policies, and legacies. Hitler and Afwerki have certain parallels in their approach to totalitarianism and their use of military force to achieve their goals. It is essential to comprehend these parallels and distinctions to comprehend the historical context and ramifications of their respective leadership styles.

Chapter 29
Possible Repetition of Past Events

Concerning the emergence of authoritarian leaders and the weakening of democratic norms and principles, there are unsettling indications that history is repeating itself in certain respects.

The emergence of populist and nationalist politicians throughout the world is one of the most prominent illustrations of this. These politicians frequently use minority groups as scapegoats and portray themselves as the saviours of their own nations. This echoes the 1930s rhetoric of fascist leaders such as Hitler, who blamed Jews and other minorities for Germany's woes.

In many nations, there has also been an increase in anti-immigrant sentiment and xenophobia, as well as a decline in regard for international human rights and humanitarian standards. This has resulted in a surge in refugee crises throughout the world as well as an increase in societal polarisation and conflict.

In certain instances, authoritarian administrations have made clear measures to destroy the free press and other democratic institutions. This has been observed in nations such as Turkey and Russia, whose respective leaders have been accused of intervening in elections and stifling opposition.

There are worrisome parallels between the current period and the emergence of fascism in the 1930s, even though there are variances. To avoid history from repeating itself, it is crucial that people throughout the world remain vigilant and speak out against authoritarianism and the deterioration of democratic principles.

Does it end?

Eritrea's condition is complicated, and it is impossible to foresee the future. Yet, there are grounds to be cautiously optimistic about the country's ultimate progress towards more stability and democracy.

One of the primary grounds for optimism is that a growing number of Eritreans are speaking out against the administration and seeking reform. Notwithstanding the dangers of speaking out, an increasing number of individuals are joining the opposition and asking for democratic reforms. This indicates that the population's desire for change is developing, which might eventually result in a substantial political transformation.

The fact that Eritrea has a young population, with a median age of just 19, is another cause for hope. This indicates that there is a huge and expanding population of young people who are more inclined to be receptive to innovative ideas and to advocate for change. As this generation becomes more politically active and involved, they may play a crucial role in moulding the destiny of the nation.

There are also indications that the international world is becoming increasingly involved in the Eritrea problem. In recent years, there have been greater calls for human rights improvements in the nation, as well as more focus on concerns such as forced labour and refugee treatment. This growing pressure from the international community may finally result in government reforms.

For the situation in Eritrea to improve, however, considerable obstacles must be surmounted. The fact that the administration has demonstrated little desire to engage in conversation or compromise with the opposition is one of the greatest barriers. This means that any advance towards democracy is likely to be gradual and incremental, as opposed to rapid and spectacular.

In addition, the country has enormous economic issues, including as high unemployment and inadequate infrastructure investment. Without major economic changes and investment, Eritrea would struggle to construct a stable and wealthy nation.

A further difficulty is that Eritrea is a small, isolated nation with scant natural resources. This suggests that it may be challenging for the nation to attract considerable international investment or to create a robust economy.

Notwithstanding these obstacles, there are indications that advancement is feasible. For instance, Eritrea and Ethiopia struck a historic peace accord in 2018, bringing an end to decades of strife between the two nations. This accord has already resulted in some improvements in ties between Eritrea and other nations in the area, which might assist in facilitating further changes.

While the overall situation in Eritrea is far from ideal, there are reasons for optimism. Eritreans can assist in laying the basis for a more peaceful and prosperous future if they continue to speak out against government abuses and advocate for democratic changes. Eritrea might emerge from its current crises and become a more open and democratic country with the assistance of the international community and a commitment to constructing a brighter future.

Milton Keynes UK
Ingram Content Group UK Ltd.
UKHW020842301123
433406UK00012B/156

9 781915 996640